AF442062

Over 55 and Alive

Michael Cook

Copyright © 2024

All Rights Reserved

Dedication

In memory of my mom, Joann Cook, a great woman who taught everyone around her how to love, be kind, and BE ALIVE, no matter what age.

Thanks for everything, Mom and Dad.

About the Author

My name is Michael Cook, and I turned 55 when I decided to write this book. I was born in Astoria, Queens, and have lived in many places throughout the United States, such as New Jersey, Washington, Utah, California, and Hawaii. I was happily married to a wonderful woman for almost 29 years. We had a traditional family life, living the American dream with a big house, four amazing kids (one boy and three girls), and two grandchildren.

From a very young age, I've been a business owner most of my life. My first business was a franchise location in the rent-to-own industry that I owned and operated. Five years later, I got licensed as a general contractor and started a multi-million-dollar construction business. A few years later, I decided to take a stab at the food business. I bought a healthy-based smoothie shop and turned it into a healthy food restaurant.

It's funny how, even with all the life experiences and time that has passed, I never really worried about my age until now. Lately, I feel overwhelmed and challenged by the idea of technically becoming a senior citizen at the age of fifty-five. So many thoughts run through my mind about things I never had to worry about before, such as my health, financial situation, and activities suitable for my age. I have had numerous thoughts running through my mind, and I do not function well that way. I enjoy making checklists. Not only does it free up my mind, but it also helps me stay organized and accomplish tasks, particularly at my age (ha-ha). Therefore, I decided to start writing them down. There are many things to consider that I never thought about before, and it turns out many people are in the same boat as me. This is my attempt at self-therapy, but I also hope it is beneficial for all of us to transition to our next chapter in life as senior citizens.

Contents

Chapter 1: Introduction

Nobody tells you exactly what it feels like when you get older. There's no guidebook for aging, which, like a biology textbook discussing puberty, details all the changes you're going to have to deal with. Sure, when you're younger, you have ideas.

"Oh, I should enjoy these physical activities while I still can."

"Before you know it, I'll be old and clutching my back in pain every time I get out of a chair."

Things like that. Or that when you're older, you'll get 'old socks' – the kind that would prevent you from slipping, falling over, and breaking the frail bones in your now-elderly body.

Still, no amount of preparation or speculation prepared me for a pivotal moment when I knew I had made it. I was opening my mail one day when some bold red lettering caught my eye. It was an invitation in my name from the American Association for Retired Persons (AARP). There it was. I was officially old.

When I use the term 'fifty-five' about age, I think it's always been something that classifies you as a pretty old person. It was something that I would look at with the view that I was far away from it and didn't have to think about it for a long time.

Well, as I approach fifty-five, a milestone often associated with becoming a senior citizen, a flood of thoughts rushed into my mind. You know, things that I never really thought much about before. I've lived through various ages, from being a young kid to a grown-up, but for some reason, hitting the number fifty-five felt so different from all the rest of the years so far.

It's like suddenly I find myself pondering about so many new things. Thoughts about my health, my financial situation, and even what I should do at this stage of life occupy my mind more than ever before. I guess it's because fifty-five seems like a big number, one that triggers a lot of changes in how I see things.

Honestly, when I got close to this age, I started feeling a bit anxious. All these thoughts kept creeping in, but you know what? Now that I'm fifty-five, it's not as scary as I thought it would be. I mean, I'm healthy, I work out, and life's not drastically different from what it was before. It's funny how we perceive certain ages based on what we've seen our parents or grandparents go through in the past.

Back then, people seemed to dress differently, and the way they carried themselves made it feel like they were almost ready to retire from life. But things have changed. Life expectancy has improved a lot. Nowadays, people are living longer, well into their 70s and 80s. So, the whole perspective on getting older is different now. That's what I've come to realize as I've hit this age myself.

You know, as I pondered over these concerns that accompany turning fifty-five, I realized the significance of addressing them head-on. It's not just about acknowledging these worries but also taking proactive steps to handle them. Because the thing is, these concerns aren't just brief thoughts—they're real and need attention.

First and foremost, I believe acknowledging these concerns is crucial. It's like shining a light on what's bothering you rather than sweeping it under the rug. By acknowledging these worries, we give ourselves a chance to confront them, understand them better, and eventually find ways to manage them.

For instance, thinking about health and mortality might seem daunting, but it's necessary. It forces us to prioritize our well-being, take better care of ourselves, and maybe adopt healthier habits. Addressing health concerns isn't about fearing what might happen; it's about being more conscious and proactive in maintaining good health. I've found that I'm suddenly more cautious about my health. I find myself making sure I stick to a good diet and maintain a regular schedule. It's not like when I was young and could take risks without much worry. Now, I'm more aware that I need to take care of myself differently.

Financial stability is another concern that can't be ignored. It's a reality check—a reminder that planning for the future is essential. It might involve reevaluating savings, investments, or even retirement plans. Addressing these financial concerns early on can ease worries and provide a more secure future. So now I've got to start thinking about the future and how I can manage my finances in a way that I can live comfortably with my family and hopefully even leave them a good inheritance for after I'm gone.

Moreover, by addressing these concerns, we gain a sense of control over our lives. It's empowering to take charge and deal with these thoughts rather than letting them hover in the background, causing unnecessary stress. It's about being in the driving seat of our lives.

What I've come to realize is that by addressing these concerns, we pave the way for a smoother transition into this new phase of life. It's like preparing ourselves mentally and emotionally for the changes that might come. It's not about eliminating worries entirely but rather finding ways to navigate them better.

Another crucial aspect is seeking support and guidance. We're not alone in facing these concerns. There are resources, whether seeking professional advice, talking to friends and family, or even reading up on similar experiences. Sometimes, sharing our worries with others helps us gain perspective and find solutions.

Ignoring these concerns won't make them disappear. It might make them even more daunting. But when we address them, we open doors to potential solutions and coping mechanisms. It's about turning these concerns into opportunities for personal growth and positive change.

The importance of addressing these concerns lies in our ability to adapt, grow, and navigate this phase of life with resilience and grace. It's about taking steps to ensure that we're better equipped to face whatever comes our way, embracing this new chapter with confidence and preparedness.

Even when you try to address aging concerns, it's still funny how your perspective on life changes as you get older. Things that never crossed your mind before, like thinking about mortality, start to creep in. Just recently, I was watching the news and saw someone my age passing away. Do you remember that really popular show, *Friends*? That's another thing that makes me feel old, the fact that it has already been nearly twenty years since it ended. Anyway, the actor who played Chandler, Mathew Perry, was 54 years old. That's one year younger than me. And it was on the news that he'd died. It made me pause and realize how unpredictable life can be. It's one of those things where you reach the age at which you start seeing people near your age dying, and that can make you think,

"Gosh, I could go at any time!"

When I was younger, such thoughts never bothered me. But now, it feels more real. The reality is more substantial than when I was thirty or forty.

And then there's this thing about embracing change. You know, change can be a bit daunting. It's like stepping into the unknown, uncertain about what lies ahead. But I've realized that embracing change is essential as we transition into this phase of life. It's about adapting to the shifts that come with age and finding ways to navigate them positively.

One significant aspect of embracing change is acknowledging that things might not be the same as they used to be. Physical limitations might surface, and certain activities we once enjoyed might need adjustments. But instead of viewing these changes as setbacks, it's about finding new ways to appreciate life.

I've come to understand that as I age, there are certain things I used to do that I might need to reconsider. Travel plans, for instance, have to be more thought-out because certain places might not be as suitable for someone my age. I can't climb mountains like I used to, you know? But that doesn't mean I can't explore other beautiful destinations or enjoy different kinds of travel experiences. It's about being open to new adventures and discovering joy in different ways.

Embracing change also involves being proactive about our health. As we age, our bodies change, and we need to adapt our habits accordingly. Taking care of our health becomes a priority, whether it's through a balanced diet, regular exercise, or even seeking medical guidance. It's about being mindful of our bodies and their evolving needs.

Additionally, embracing change means being flexible in our thinking and lifestyle. It's about being open to new ideas, learning new things, and not being stuck in our ways. Adapting to changing circumstances allows us to remain relevant and engaged in life, contributing positively to our overall well-being.

Ultimately, it isn't about denying the challenges that come with aging; it's about facing them with resilience and a positive attitude. It's about understanding that change is inevitable but how we embrace it determines our journey ahead. And I believe that embracing change can make this new chapter of life fulfilling and meaningful.

But embracing change isn't just about physical limitations. It's also about the psychological shift that comes with getting older. It's about letting go of the mindset that getting older means being limited and finding opportunities for growth and fulfillment. Accepting this age and embracing it positively is something I find important. It's like finding a balance between acknowledging the changes while still staying hopeful and optimistic.

That's why, even though I spoke of my anxiousness about my age, I wanted to talk about the lighter side of getting older. Some benefits are nice, like when I received my AARP invitation, which gives me access to a range of offers and discounts *because* I am now over a certain age. It's ironic, you know? On the one hand, I get access to AARP discounts, but on the other hand, it's a reminder that I'm officially part of the senior citizen club. In a way, it's like a consolation prize saying,

"Well, you're old now. Have a discount!"

In spite of all these thoughts and considerations, I firmly believe there's hope and positivity in aging. It's not just about limitations; it's also about the opportunities to live a fuller and healthier life by being more conscious of our health choices and embracing the changes that come our way.

And I'm not saying I am some saint regarding these things. I have some friends that have it worse off, for sure. They have to take ten to twenty medications or prescriptions a day just to keep going. Me? I'm just as bad, but I take a lot of supplements and vitamins. And I take them to prevent illnesses, not because my life depends on it.

I don't want to pretend that I have it all figured out, that I've unlocked the secret to dealing with getting older— I haven't. I have had so many thoughts running through my head about all this. And the best way I deal with that is by writing things down. So, consider this book my personal checklist of things to consider when you're getting on in life, and maybe you and I can figure this aging thing out together.

Chapter 2: Health Concerns

"Growing old is not a disease. It is a natural phenomenon like the changing seasons. To age gracefully is to accept the changes with humor, good food, good friends, and a comfortable chair or two."

-Gabrielle Siddon Walker

In the spirit of Walker's insightful perspective, aging is not to be viewed as a deterioration but as a natural progression, much like the changing seasons. Embracing this transition with humor, nourishing food, cherished friendships, and a comfortable space mirrors the essence of aging gracefully. This outlook encourages a positive approach to the journey of growing older, where acceptance and appreciation for the experiences that come with age become integral to one's well-being.

Maintaining good health as a senior citizen is essential for tackling the unique challenges and changes associated with the aging process. It's like climbing a new mountain - you need to be physically and mentally prepared to handle the different terrains and obstacles you'll encounter along the way. Adopting a healthy lifestyle becomes particularly crucial in ensuring overall well-being during these later years.

Physical well-being, the foundation of senior health, can be likened to the sturdy hiking boots that support your every step. Regular, moderate exercise, such as daily walks or light yoga, plays a pivotal role in preserving flexibility, balance, and strength. These activities are not just about mobility; they serve as preventive measures against common concerns for older individuals, significantly reducing the risk of falls and injuries that can often be more severe in later stages of life.

Moreover, engaging in enjoyable physical activities, such as swimming or dancing, can further enrich your exercise routine. These activities not only diversify your workouts but also contribute to the holistic well-being. Swimming, with its low-impact nature, is gentle on joints, promoting cardiovascular health without placing undue stress. Similarly, dancing not only provides a delightful form of exercise but also enhances cognitive function by incorporating coordination and memory elements, thereby supporting both physical and mental well-being.

A balanced and nutritious diet stands as another vital component in the pursuit of senior well-being, akin to the fuel that keeps you going on your climb. This extends beyond a mere comparison, emphasizing that just as fuel powers a journey, a well-balanced diet fuels the body and mind for the journey through aging. Integrating a variety of fruits, vegetables, lean proteins, and whole grains into daily meals is akin to supplying the essential nutrients that nourish your body and mind, playing a pivotal role in managing weight and promoting overall health.

Much like adequate hydration is crucial during a physical climb; it is a vital element in the journey of aging. Hydration is like the water that keeps you refreshed and energized throughout the climb. Beyond quenching thirst, staying adequately hydrated fosters proper digestion, supports joint health, and prevents issues like constipation that can often become more prevalent with age. It serves as a fundamental aspect of maintaining bodily functions and ensuring that each step taken is supported by a well-nourished and well-hydrated body.

Cognitive health, akin to the map and compass guiding your journey, emerges as another critical aspect for seniors. This underlines the importance of mental acuity in traversing the challenges of aging. Engaging in mentally stimulating activities becomes the road map that ensures cognitive resilience. Activities such as reading, solving puzzles, or playing brain games play a pivotal role in keeping your mind sharp. Much like a well-used map, these activities become tools that reduce the risk of cognitive decline and conditions like dementia, providing a clear path for cognitive well-being.

Moreover, this extends to the practice of mindfulness techniques, which can be likened to the compass that helps you maintain direction and purpose. Mindfulness, particularly through activities like meditation, becomes a guiding force for both mental and emotional well-being. Just as a compass points toward true north, mindfulness helps individuals align with a sense of clarity and emotional balance. The benefits extend beyond cognitive health, impacting overall well-being and contributing to a more resilient and fulfilling journey through the senior years.

In the holistic approach to senior health, the incorporation of mentally stimulating activities and mindfulness techniques becomes an integral part of the strategy. Together with physical exercise and a balanced diet, these elements form a comprehensive toolkit, ensuring that seniors set out on their journey with not just physical strength and nutritional support but also with mental acuity and emotional well-being. This multifaceted approach ensures that the journey through the golden years is not only sustained but also enriched by cognitive vitality and emotional balance.

Regular health check-ups stand as indispensable pillars for the early detection and effective management of potential health issues, much like pit stops ensure your equipment is in optimal condition during a journey. This emphasizes the proactive and preventive nature of health check-ups, positioning them as essential checkpoints that play a crucial role in maintaining overall health for seniors.

Imagine these routine medical appointments as comprehensive check-ins on the well-being of your body, much like inspecting the various components of a vehicle during a pit stop. Attending these appointments becomes a proactive approach, allowing healthcare professionals to identify any emerging health concerns promptly. It is a preventive measure that aims not only to detect issues early but also to address them effectively, contributing to better overall health outcomes for seniors.

Participating in recommended screenings can be compared to diagnostics during a pit stop, providing a thorough assessment of your health status. This proactive engagement ensures that potential problems are identified before they escalate, promoting a sense of control over one's health journey. Additionally, staying up-to-date with vaccinations acts as a preventive measure, creating a shield against potential health threats, much like ensuring your vehicle is equipped with the latest safety features.

Beyond physical and cognitive well-being, emotional health emerges as another crucial aspect in shaping a senior's overall quality of life. It can be likened to the sunshine that warmly envelops your spirit, lifting your mood and brightening your days. Acknowledging and nurturing emotional well-being is integral to a holistic approach to senior health.

Imagine emotional health as the radiant sunshine that not only adds warmth but also cultivates a positive outlook. Maintaining a robust social network becomes the avenue through which this sunshine permeates one's life. This network, comprising supportive friends and family, acts as a buffer against the shadows of loneliness and contributes to a sense of emotional well-being. Much like sunshine dispels darkness, a strong social support system helps alleviate feelings of isolation and reduces the risk of depression, fostering a brighter emotional realm for seniors.

Staying socially connected is the key to harnessing the positive energy of emotional well-being. Participating in community activities, attending family gatherings, and nurturing friendships are like the rays of sunlight that continually nourish and invigorate. These social connections significantly contribute to a fulfilling and happier life, reinforcing the importance of a well-rounded and emotionally satisfying existence.

Managing chronic conditions becomes increasingly vital in senior health, like unexpected deviations on your journey. Many seniors grapple with conditions like hypertension, diabetes, or arthritis. Adhering to prescribed medications, monitoring your health, and making necessary lifestyle adjustments are crucial components of managing these conditions effectively. By taking proactive steps, seniors can optimize their health and maintain a higher quality of life, fostering resilience in the face of health challenges. This proactive stance allows seniors to embrace their later years with vitality and purpose.

Maintaining good health is not a race; it's a journey, a continuous dance with life's ever-changing rhythm. Embrace each step, nourish each aspect of your being, and craft your own vibrant journey of senior health. It's a rewarding adventure that will lead you to a summit of well-being and fulfillment.

Comprehensive Health Guide for Seniors

Maintaining optimal health is paramount for individuals aged 55 and above as they surmount the distinct challenges associated with the aging process. Adopting a proactive and holistic approach to health becomes increasingly crucial during these later years. Here is the comprehensive guide that explores practical tips and strategies designed to assist senior individuals in addressing their health needs. From incorporating regular exercise routines to embracing balanced nutrition, from prioritizing regular health check-ups to ensuring adequate sleep, these guidelines aim to empower seniors to enhance their overall well-being and lead fulfilling lives.

1. Regular Exercise

Integrate a variety of exercises into your routine, combing aerobic, strength, and flexibility activities for holistic well-being. Activities like walking, swimming, and yoga are optimal choices, promoting cardiovascular health, preserving muscle strength, and enhancing overall flexibility. Strive for a minimum of 150 minutes of moderate-intensity exercise weekly, fostering a balanced approach to physical fitness. Consistent physical activity not only aids in weight management and lowering the risk of chronic conditions but also uplifts mood and enhances the quality of sleep. Embrace this well-rounded exercise routine to support your overall health and vitality.

2. Balanced Nutrition

Embrace a well-rounded diet that prioritizes fruits, vegetables, whole grains, and lean proteins to foster comprehensive health. Ensuring sufficient intake of calcium and vitamin D is crucial for maintaining robust bones, while staying adequately hydrated is equally fundamental for overall well-being. Choose nutrient-dense foods to address specific nutritional needs associated with aging and support vital bodily functions. For personalized dietary guidance, consider consulting a nutritionist who can provide advice to meet your individual requirements. By making informed dietary choices, you empower yourself to maintain optimal health, enhance energy levels, and fortify your body against the effects of aging.

4. Adequate Sleep

Sleep is the golden chain that ties health and our bodies together. Ensure you consistently achieve 7-9 hours of quality sleep each night. Quality sleep is integral to overall well-being, contributing to cognitive function, mood regulation, and immune system support. Establish a bedtime routine and create a sleep-friendly environment to cultivate healthy sleep patterns. If persistent sleep issues arise, consult with a sleep specialist to address potential sleep disorders and optimize your sleep quality. This proactive approach not only enhances your daily functioning but also contributes to long-term health benefits. Embrace the power of a good night's sleep as a fundamental pillar of your well-rounded health contributes routine, promoting resilience and energy in your everyday life.

5. Stay Socially Engaged

Cultivate your mental and emotional well-being by maintaining robust social connections. Participate in activities that bring joy and prioritize regular, quality time with loved ones. Social interactions play a pivotal role in fostering a sense of belonging and purpose, particularly in later years. Explore community groups, clubs, or volunteering opportunities to actively engage with others and contribute to your community. Building and sustaining social relationships not only enrich your life but also act as a protective factor against feelings of isolation and loneliness. Embrace the power of social engagement as an essential aspect of your holistic well-being, cultivating a vibrant network of connections that positively impact your mental and emotional health throughout life.

6. Manage Stress

Prioritize your overall well-being by integrating stress-reducing practices into your daily routine. Engage in activities like meditation, deep breathing exercises, or indulging in hobbies that bring relaxation, creating a buffer against the detrimental effects of chronic stress on both physical and mental health. Acknowledge that effective stress management is integral to a balanced and healthy life. Explore mindfulness techniques or consider joining stress management programs to develop personalized coping strategies that align with your lifestyle. By actively managing stress, you not only enhance your resilience but also create a foundation for sustained well-being. Embrace these practices as essential components of your holistic health routine, fostering a sense of calm and equilibrium that positively influences various aspects of your life.

7. Limit Alcohol and Quit Smoking

For better health, adopt mindful habits such as moderating alcohol consumption and taking a transformative step to quit smoking. Stopping tobacco use markedly diminishes the risk of associated health issues, contributing to an overall sense of well-being. If you are working toward quitting smoking, seek support from healthcare professionals, support groups, or specialized cessation programs to increase your chances of success. By limiting alcohol intake and eliminating tobacco use, you make substantial strides toward improving cardiovascular health and establishing a foundation for comprehensive well-being. These choices empower you to embrace a healthier lifestyle, reducing the impact of harmful habits and fostering a positive trajectory for your long-term health journey.

8. Regular Vision and Hearing Checks

Nurture your sensory well-being through regular vision and hearing checks. Timely detection and intervention for changes in these senses enhance safety and contribute to an improved quality of life. Schedule comprehensive eye exams and hearing tests at recommended intervals, promptly addressing any concerns or changes in sensory function. If prescribed, consider using corrective lenses or hearing aids to optimize your sensory experiences, supporting independence in daily activities. Embrace these proactive measures to ensure that your vision and hearing remain integral components of your overall health and well-being. Regular check-ups for these crucial senses contribute to a lifestyle that values preventive care, enabling you to experience the world with confidence and clarity.

9. Brain Health

Cultivate your cognitive well-being by regularly challenging your brain through activities like puzzles, reading, or acquiring new skills. Maintaining mental activity is crucial for sustaining cognitive function and promoting a healthy brain. Integrate brain-training activities into your routine, such as crossword puzzles, memory games, or educational courses. Moreover, prioritize social engagement, as meaningful interactions stimulate cognitive processes and contribute to overall brain health. These practices stand as foundational pillars for preserving your cognitive vitality and well-being, fostering a sharper and more resilient mind. Embrace the holistic approach to brain health, where mental stimulation and social connections work synergistically to enhance your cognitive resilience, ensuring a fulfilling and cognitively vibrant life.

10. Preventive Measures

Take proactive steps to safeguard your health through vaccinations and preventive measures. Use sunscreen to protect your skin and practice good hygiene to prevent infections. Stay informed about vaccination schedules and preventive healthcare measures by discussing them with your healthcare provider. These measures are vital in preventing potential illnesses and maintaining overall health. Additionally, adopt good hygiene habits, including regular handwashing and proper sanitation, to minimize the risk of infections and provide comprehensive support for your well-being. Stay committed to these preventive measures for a healthier and more resilient future.

It's never too late to adopt healthy habits. Small, consistent changes can make a significant impact on your health and well-being after the age of 55. Whether it's adding a daily walk, swapping sugary drinks for water, or prioritizing a few minutes of mindfulness, every positive step counts.

Consulting Your Healthcare Professional for Personalized Advice

Consulting your healthcare professional is foundational for proactive health management. This personalized approach addresses the unique aspects of your health, tailoring recommendations to your individual needs and fostering collaboration between you and your healthcare provider. It provides a comprehensive understanding of your health history, identifying risk factors and genetic predispositions.

Regular check-ups with your healthcare provider are invaluable opportunities for ongoing personalized care. These appointments go beyond addressing immediate concerns; they serve as proactive measures to detect potential issues early on. Through thorough assessments, screenings, and discussions about your lifestyle, your healthcare professional can identify subtle changes and offer guidance to mitigate potential health risks before they escalate. Investing time in preventive care fosters a proactive approach to your well-being, enhancing the likelihood of maintaining optimal health and preventing the development of serious medical conditions. Prioritizing these check-ups ensures a comprehensive and personalized healthcare strategy.

Furthermore, a personalized approach extends to medication management. Your healthcare provider, armed with knowledge about your medical history and current conditions, can prescribe medications that align with your unique health profile. This minimizes the risk of adverse reactions, ensures optimal efficacy, and allows for adjustments based on your individual response to treatments. Investing time in preventive care fosters a proactive approach to your well-being, enhancing the likelihood of maintaining optimal health and preventing the development of serious medical conditions. Prioritizing these check-ups ensures a comprehensive and tailored healthcare strategy.

For individuals grappling with chronic conditions like diabetes, hypertension, or arthritis, personalized advice is paramount. Your healthcare professional emerges as a vital ally in addressing the complexities of these conditions. They not only customize management strategies but also offer lifestyle recommendations, fostering an active role in your health journey. This ongoing support empowers you to make informed decisions, ensuring a collaborative and effective approach to managing your chronic health challenges.

Preventive care is pivotal in personalized advice, focusing on sustaining a healthy lifestyle and avoiding potential health issues. Engaging in conversations about your health habits, diet, and exercise routines allows your healthcare provider to give recommendations to your goals, fostering overall well-being. This proactive approach not only identifies risks but empowers you with strategies to mitigate them. Integrating preventive measures into your daily life enhances the quality of healthcare, emphasizing the significance of early intervention and lifestyle adjustments.

Staying informed is another key benefit of personalized advice. In the ever-evolving world of healthcare, your healthcare professional serves as a reliable source of up-to-date information. They can guide you on vaccinations, screenings, and health guidelines that are specifically relevant to your age, gender, and medical history. This ensures that you remain actively engaged in preventive measures and are equipped with the knowledge needed to make informed decisions about your health. With personalized advice, you gain a proactive approach to your well-being, fostering a sense of empowerment and confidence in going through the complexities of your unique health journey.

In essence, the significance of consulting your healthcare professional for personalized advice goes beyond addressing immediate health concerns. It encompasses a proactive, collaborative, and holistic approach to your well-being. By fostering a strong relationship with your healthcare provider, you not only gain access to personalized recommendations but also actively participate in the journey toward optimal health. This ongoing collaboration forms the backbone of a healthcare strategy that is tailored to you, promoting long-term wellness and a fulfilling life.

Chapter 3: Aging & Society

"Age is an issue of mind over matter. If you don't mind, it doesn't matter," famously said Mark Twain, aptly capturing the evolving social attitudes toward individuals aged 55 and above. In recent times, many societies have observed a noticeable change, acknowledging the substantial inputs that older individuals bring to their communities. The notion of "dynamic aging" has gained ground, underlining the significance of seniors engaging in various aspects of life, including employment, volunteer work, and social engagements. This shift in outlook has resulted in a growing recognition of the expertise and sagacity that older individuals provide.

Despite these positive transformations, ageism, or discrimination rooted in age, continues to be a substantial concern. Unfavorable stereotypes and prejudices against older individuals can detrimentally influence their job opportunities, access to healthcare, and societal perception. A collective attempt is being made to challenge these stereotypes and promote inclusiveness, highlighting that individuals over 55 represent a diverse collective with distinctive skills, passions, and capabilities. Furthermore, the promotion of interactions between different age groups is aiding in the creation of better comprehension and admiration, leading to a more united and supportive society.

The worldwide trend of an aging population is inciting discussions regarding policies and infrastructure to cater to the requirements of seniors. This encompasses making public areas more easily accessible and modifying healthcare services for the elderly. This growing awareness stresses the importance of establishing environments that are welcoming to older individuals. While progress has been made, maintaining a focus on age-associated stereotypes and making certain that extensive support systems are in place remains crucial for fostering more favorable and inclusive societal attitudes toward senior citizens.

In the workplace, older adults frequently encounter difficulties in securing employment or progressing in their careers because of biases related to age. This issue is especially evident in sectors that usually prefer younger employees, such as the technology and entertainment industries. To counter this, some organizations are implementing programs that emphasize diversity and inclusion concerning age. These endeavors seek to form a more balanced workforce and leverage the distinct outlooks and experiences that older personnel bring.

Imagine a scenario in which an advertising company, traditionally controlled by younger creatives, recruits a senior marketing strategist in her late 60s. Her appointment initially raises questions, but she swiftly demonstrates insights and a fresh approach to campaigns that resonate with a broader audience. Her ability to integrate conventional marketing strategies with modern digital trends transforms the company's approach, resulting in enhanced success and a more varied client base. This highlights the worth of experience and the innovative potential that can arise from challenging ageist stereotypes in the workplace.

Healthcare is another field where the repercussions of aging populations are observable. As people live longer, the demand for healthcare services made to the specific necessities of seniors is on the rise. This has resulted in the growth of geriatric medicine and an emphasis on preventive care to preserve health and well-being during later years. However, there is still a requirement for wider access to these specialized services, particularly in underserved communities.

Regarding social participation, numerous seniors are defying stereotypes by remaining actively engaged in their communities. They are not merely passive recipients of care but are actively contributing through volunteering, mentoring, and even establishing new businesses. This dynamic involvement enriches communities and bestows a sense of purpose and connection upon seniors. As John F. Kennedy once expressed, *'One person can make a difference, and everyone should try.'*

One inspiring example is Susan, a 70-year-old retired school teacher. Following her retirement, Susan did not wish to relax at home; instead, she aspired to make a positive impact. Consequently, she initiated a community garden project in her small town.

Susan's project commenced as a modest piece of land, but it swiftly expanded into a flourishing community garden. She rallied other seniors, as well as individuals of all age groups, to join. They cultivated various vegetables and herbs, distributed the produce amongst volunteers and donated to local food banks. This garden evolved into more than a mere source of fresh produce; it transformed into a community hub where people could congregate, share anecdotes, and acquire knowledge from each other.

Through her initiative, Susan demonstrated that age does not present a barrier to contributing significantly to society. She employed her organizational skills and her passion for gardening to unite individuals. The garden not only enhanced the town's access to fresh sustenance but also evolved into a site for intergenerational learning and bonding. Younger volunteers acquired knowledge about gardening and the significance of community service, while older participants relished physical activity, social interaction, and the gratification of mentoring others. Susan's story exemplifies how seniors can assume an active and indispensable role in their communities.

The function of technology in improving the lives of older adults is also gaining recognition. From applications that promote health supervision to social platforms that facilitate connections with family and friends, technology plays a crucial role in aiding the autonomy and involvement of seniors. Nonetheless, it is imperative to ensure that these technologies are accessible and user-friendly for older individuals.

Housing is another critical aspect of supporting an aging population. There is a growing inclination toward making living spaces that are accommodating for seniors, ensuring they are secure, comfortable, and conducive to a high quality of life. This encompasses not only specialized retirement communities but also adjustments to existing residences to make them more age-friendly.

Additionally, the contribution of seniors to the realm of arts and culture is noteworthy. Many older individuals join in artistic endeavors through writing, painting, music, or other forms of expression. These pursuits not only provide a channel for creativity but also augment the cultural diversity of a society.

Education and continuous learning are additional realms in which seniors are actively involved. Numerous universities and community colleges provide programs specifically tailored for older learners. These programs offer opportunities for personal development, skill enhancement, and intellectual stimulation.

Intergenerational initiatives are also playing a pivotal role in bridging the gap between the young and the old. By bringing together different age groups, these programs promote mutual understanding and respect. They provide avenues for older adults to share their wisdom and experiences, while younger individuals can offer fresh viewpoints and technological expertise.

Lastly, the role of government and policy in supporting an aging population is of paramount importance. Policies that advocate age inclusiveness, safeguard against discrimination, and deliver assistance for healthcare, housing, and social services are essential. Governments across the globe are recognizing the need to adapt their policies to accommodate shifting demographics and ensure that older individuals can continue leading meaningful, active lives.

Although obstacles persist, the evolving societal attitudes toward individuals aged 55 and above are encouraging. The recognition of their valuable contributions and the endeavors to create more inclusive, supportive surroundings reflect a favorable transformation in how society perceives aging. As the population continues to age, it will be progressively critical to sustain these efforts and guarantee that older individuals can remain active, esteemed members of society.

The Evolution of Aging

Across various cultures, the perception of aging has evolved, reflecting a complex relationship of historical, social, and economic factors. Despite these changes, a significant emphasis remains on youth and youthful age. This emphasis is not uniform across all societies; it varies in intensity and expression. Here let's delve into the key points to know thorough understanding of this subject.

1. Obsession with Youth

The obsession with youth in many societies, particularly in Western regions, is not just a superficial trend; it is deeply ingrained in the cultural fabric. This fixation permeates various aspects of life, from employment practices to everyday social interactions. In the entertainment industry, for example, it's common to see older actors using makeup and visual effects to appear younger, reinforcing the idea that youth equates to desirability. The fashion industry also plays a role, often showcasing clothing and trends primarily on young models, creating a perception that style is exclusive to the young.

In the corporate world, the emphasis on youth often translates into a preference for hiring younger employees, with the assumption that they are more adaptable and tech-savvy. This can lead to older workers feeling undervalued or pressured to keep up with their younger counterparts, sometimes going to great lengths to mask their age. Furthermore, the prevalence of anti-aging products in everyday life—from skincare to health supplements—underlines a society that views aging as a problem to be solved, rather than a natural process to be embraced.

It not only impacts the self-esteem of older individuals but also leads to a loss of intergenerational knowledge and experience in various fields. By constantly highlighting youth as the ideal state, society risks undervaluing the depth, resilience, and wisdom that come with aging.

2. Ageism

Ageism, the discrimination against individuals based on their age, is a deeply entrenched issue that affects numerous aspects of life. Beyond the workplace, it's evident in the entertainment industry, where older actors are often relegated to roles that reinforce stereotypes about aging. In healthcare, ageism manifests in the prioritization of treatments for younger patients, sometimes leading to inadequate care for older adults. In the realm of technology, the rapid pace of change can alienate older individuals, creating a divide where they feel left behind by the digital revolution.

In social settings, ageism can lead to older adults being excluded from mainstream conversations and activities, reinforcing a sense of isolation. This is particularly evident in the portrayal of older individuals in media, where they are often depicted in contexts of decline or dependency rather than as active, contributing members of society. Such portrayals contribute to a societal narrative that undervalues and marginalizes older individuals, perpetuating stereotypes and leading to a diminished sense of worth and belonging.

3. The Beauty Industry's Role

The beauty industry plays a significant role in reinforcing social fears about aging. The industry's focus on anti-aging products perpetuates the notion that aging is undesirable and must be combated. This is evident in the marketing strategies of beauty brands, which often use language and imagery that equate youth with beauty and success. The industry's influence extends beyond cosmetics, influencing fashion and lifestyle choices, where aging is portrayed as a condition to be concealed.

This approach has profound implications, particularly for women, who are often the primary target of anti-aging campaigns. It contributes to societal pressure where aging is viewed as a failure, leading many to pursue expensive and sometimes harmful procedures to maintain a youthful appearance. The beauty industry's narrow focus on youth as the standard of beauty neglects the natural diversity of aging, reinforcing a cycle of ageism and self-doubt.

4. Social Media's Unrealistic Standards

The impact of social media on social attitudes toward aging is significant. Platforms like Instagram and Facebook are flooded with images that promote a youthful, idealized lifestyle, often heavily edited to remove any signs of aging. This creates an unrealistic standard that can be particularly damaging for older individuals, who may feel that they don't measure up to these portrayed ideals.

The trend of sharing 'anti-aging' tips and products on social media further perpetuates the idea that aging is something to be resisted. This not only affects self-perception but also influences how aging is viewed in the broader societal context. The constant exposure to these ideals can lead to a distorted view of aging, where natural changes are seen as flaws rather than a normal part of life.

5. Positive Aging Movements

Positive aging movements have emerged as a powerful response to the challenges posed by societal attitudes toward aging. These movements are gaining significant momentum, advocating for a more balanced and accepting view of aging. They encompass a wide range of initiatives, such as campaigns featuring older models in fashion and beauty industries, challenging the traditional narrative that beauty is exclusive to youth. For instance, fashion brands that include models in their 60s and 70s in their advertising campaigns help to normalize aging and showcase it as a period of continued vibrancy and style.

These movements also celebrate the achievements of older individuals across various fields. Recognition of older professionals' contributions in areas like science, literature, and public service highlights the continued potential and productivity of individuals well past the conventional retirement age. This serves to break down the stereotype that aging equates to a decrease in relevance or capability.

Support groups and community programs play a crucial role in these movements. They provide spaces for older adults to explore new interests, hobbies, and social connections. For example, art classes, technology workshops, and group travel opportunities designed for older adults help foster a sense of community and continued growth. These activities not only provide enjoyment and learning but also combat isolation and support mental health.

6. Mental Health Impacts

The societal stress of maintaining a younger look could have profound and enduring effects on mental health. This strain is in particular reported among the ones over fifty-five, who might also feel marginalized through a lifestyle that idealizes youngsters. The pressure of trying to conform to those beliefs can bring about various mental health issues, consisting of tension, melancholy, and a diminished experience of self-worth.

For instance, consider a scenario where an individual in their late fifties starts to withdraw from social activities they once enjoyed due to feelings of self-consciousness about their aging appearance. Such withdrawal can lead to social isolation, exacerbating emotions of loneliness and despair. It's vital for society to understand these mental health influences and try to create environments where aging is portrayed positively. This includes promoting media and advertising content material that incorporates more numerous varieties of a while, thereby helping to normalize aging and lessen the stigma attached to it.

7. Embracing Healthy Aging

Healthy aging is not just about maintaining physical health; it encompasses mental and emotional well-being, too. It's about accepting the aging process and finding ways to support health and happiness at every stage of life. A holistic approach to healthy aging involves focusing on activities that promote overall health, such as engaging in physical exercise, eating a nutritious diet, and maintaining strong social connections.

A great example of embracing healthy aging is community centers offering a range of activities tailored to older adults. These might include yoga classes designed for senior flexibility, book clubs that stimulate mental activity and provide social interaction, or cooking classes that teach how to prepare nutritious meals suitable for older adults. These activities help shift the focus from trying to look younger to enhancing quality of life and well-being in the aging process.

By embracing these positive aging movements, recognizing the mental health impacts of ageism, and promoting a holistic approach to healthy aging, society can move toward a more age-inclusive and respectful culture. This shift is essential for creating a supportive environment where aging is celebrated as a natural and enriching phase of life.

8. Lifestyle Choices for Better Aging

Lifestyle choices are crucial in determining the quality of life as people age. Engaging in physical activity, maintaining a balanced diet, and having an active social life are key to aging well. Regular exercise, for instance, not only improves physical health but also enhances mental well-being. Participating in social activities, whether it's community events, clubs, or volunteering, helps maintain a sense of connection and purpose.

The diet also plays a vital role in aging healthily. Eating a diet rich in fruits, vegetables, whole grains, and lean proteins can help manage age-related health issues and contribute to overall vitality. Additionally, staying mentally active through hobbies, learning new skills, or engaging in intellectual pursuits can help keep the mind sharp and reduce the risk of cognitive decline.

By focusing on these lifestyle choices, individuals can not only enhance their quality of life as they age but also challenge the societal norms that equate aging with decline. Embracing a lifestyle that prioritizes health and well-being over a youthful appearance can lead to a more fulfilling and enjoyable aging experience.

Challenging Social Norms and Shaping Perspectives

"Have you ever paused to question the societal norms that surround aging?" What if, instead of resisting the natural progression of time, we embraced the beauty that comes with it? In a world constantly chasing youthfulness, there's an unexplored realm of wisdom and grace that accompanies aging. It's a journey often overlooked, yet it holds the potential to redefine our perspectives on life.

In our relentless pursuit of eternal youth, we inadvertently perpetuate the notion that aging is a battle to be fought rather than a chapter to be celebrated. Society bombards us with images and messages that suggest youth is the pinnacle of existence, leaving little room for appreciation of the nuanced beauty that unfolds with age.

When we journey through the maze of life, we encounter an array of experiences that shape us into complex beings. Each wrinkle etched on our faces tells a story, evidence of the resilience and adaptability that characterizes the human spirit. Yet, in a culture that often highlights external appearances, these lines are often seen as blemishes rather than marks of wisdom earned through the journey of living.

It's a conundrum we face — the paradoxical nature of societal expectations. On the one hand, we are urged to set out on a perpetual voyage in pursuit of the elusive fountain of youth, while on the other, we are reminded that with age comes a certain transcendence, a liberation from the confines of societal expectations. The question then becomes: Can we undo the deeply ingrained beliefs that stigmatize aging and embrace the full spectrum of what it means to grow old?

Aging is not just a physical transformation; it is a profound transformation of the soul. It involves an interplay of experiences, relationships, and self-discovery. Yet, we are often spellbound by the complex structures of ageism, where the worth of an individual is measured by the number of years they've circled the sun.

In challenging societal norms, it is essential to go into the rich perspectives that make up the web of our collective consciousness. The older generation holds within them a wealth of knowledge, a ground of stories that span decades. Their voices, often overlooked, capture the essence of resilience, love, loss, and the undying human spirit.

Embracing the beauty of aging is not a call to resign from the endeavor of self-improvement or growth. It is, instead, an invitation to shift the narrative, to recognize that the pursuit of personal development is not confined to the bounds of youth. It is a lifelong journey, an ongoing venture that traverses the ups and downs of existence.

Let's highlight intergenerational relationships and value the wisdom of older generations to create an inclusive society. Aging is a journey of joys, sorrows, victories, and defeats that add depth of character. To redefine aging, we should challenge ageist stereotypes and use language that celebrates growth and experience. This cultural shift requires reassessing values and perceptions. Let's embrace the beauty of aging, which evolves and matures like a fine wine, encompassing all colors, including silver and gray.

The Impact of Living Environments on Aging

Living conditions have a big impact on people's daily experiences, ability to get healthcare, social opportunities, and general well-being as they get older.

Urban environments are rich in resources that can improve the quality of life for senior citizens. These resources include a wide range of healthcare facilities, cultural events, and social gathering places. Urban inhabitants are fortunate to have access to a variety of social venues and specialized medical treatment, which offer crucial support networks. However, the advantages of urban living come with challenges, such as higher living costs, noise, and air pollution. Additionally, the bustling pace of city life can sometimes lead to feelings of isolation among older adults despite being surrounded by a large population.

For older people, suburban surroundings typically provide a more balanced existence. These places usually blend the peace and space more typical of rural settings with the accessibility of basic services seen in urban areas. Parks, community centers, and recreational facilities are common in the suburbs and encourage an active and socially engaged lifestyle. However, many suburban regions' reliance on private transportation might provide a challenge for people who no longer drive, possibly isolating them. Even though suburban healthcare is often better than urban healthcare, it could not be as specialized or as widely available.

Rural settings grant a distinct experience marked by tight-knit communities and a deep link to nature's bounty. The tranquility and leisurely pace of rural life can benefit the elderly well-being, offering a sense of peace and engagement with neighbors. However, rural inhabitants regularly face meaningful barriers, including constrained access to medical services, with fewer clinics and experts available. Social opportunities and services such as public transportation are also less accessible in rural areas, which can further compound the challenges of isolation and accessing care.

The socioeconomic backdrop of aging emphasizes how critical it is to attend to older individuals' various demands in a variety of settings. The accessibility and tranquility of suburban living may appeal to middle-class and upper-class individuals, but there are differences between urban and rural residents' quality of life, social support, and access to healthcare that must be acknowledged and addressed. This calls for an all-encompassing strategy that takes into account the particular benefits and challenges found in each setting, with the goal of making sure that older persons, regardless of where they live, have access to the resources and assistance they need to age with dignity and quality of life.

To address these disparities, community networks and support systems that might lessen the difficulties older individuals encounter in a variety of living situations must be fostered in addition to infrastructural and service improvements. Society can better serve its aging population and make sure that everyone has the chance to have a happy and active life in their older years by adopting a more inclusive perspective on aging that considers the wide spectrum of experiences formed by one's environment.

Chapter 4: Financial Worries

At the age of 55, people often experience a significant shift in their life's journey. This stage is not merely a prelude to retirement but a crucial phase of preparation and adjustment. It's a time when the years of hard work and savings are reviewed with a new perspective, focusing on the future and the kind of life one envisions in the coming years. The approach goes beyond merely assessing the current state of finances. It's a deeper, more comprehensive analysis of how well-prepared one is for the years post-retirement, taking into account the longer lifespans people now enjoy.

This period demands a thorough examination of financial assets, retirement accounts, and other investments. It involves a careful examination of one's accumulated assets and deciding how these resources will underpin a secure and enduring lifestyle during retirement years. This evaluation isn't merely a hasty overview of figures; it's an analysis of how these funds are projected to perform in the future and their alignment with the desired lifestyle post-retirement.

Consider the scenario of an individual like John, who, upon reaching 55, takes a closer examination of his finances. John's portfolio, heavily inclined toward stocks, reflects a strategy that was suitable during his younger years, characterized by greater risk tolerance and a longer recovery period for market fluctuations. However, as retirement approaches, this allocation poses more risk than John is comfortable with. Acknowledged and addressed, this prompts John to reshape his portfolio, shifting focus to more stable investments like bonds and fixed-income assets. This change is not just about reducing risk; it's about adapting to a new phase in life, where the preservation of capital becomes as important as its growth.

Such strategic shifts are essential for financial planning at this age. They reflect a fundamental change in one's approach to risk as retirement nears. The objective is to shield the accumulated wealth throughout one's life from the immediate fluctuations of the market while ensuring the asset pool grows at a rate that surpasses inflation. Achieving this balance is vital for preserving fiscal wellness during retirement.

As people reach their mid-50s, the idea of retirement transforms from a distant possibility to an imminent certainty, prompting a shift from simple reflection on life after retirement to the development of concrete fiscal strategies. This transition marks a point where dreams and aspirations begin to shape and inform practical financial decisions. It's at this stage that the focus intensifies on effective planning methods to ensure that the envisioned retirement lifestyle is not only achievable but also sustainable. With an eye toward the future, the strategies for financial planning become more than just theoretical concepts; they transform into actionable steps designed to secure a comfortable and fulfilling retirement.

Strategies To Address Financial Planning

"A good financial plan is a road map that shows us exactly how the choices we make today will affect our future"

-Alexa Von Tobel.

Planning for retirement is a dynamic and multi-layered process that goes beyond simple savings. It requires careful consideration of retirement funds and asset management, customized to each person's distinct fiscal situation. This process is not merely about choosing suitable investment options; it also involves constant adjustment and refinement of these choices to keep pace with changing financial objectives, life transitions, and variable market trends.

As one progresses through various life phases, priorities evolve, necessitating adjustments in retirement planning methods. This method demands knowledge of different investment options and their effects on long-term economic stability. It also includes finding a balance between risk and certainty, ensuring that investments match both immediate needs and future goals.

Effective retirement planning is not a set-and-forget task. It requires continuous reevaluation to ascertain that investment portfolios, savings schemes, and other monetary choices stay pertinent and effective amidst economic shifts, personal life changes, and adjustments in regulations. This perpetual process is crucial for developing a retirement plan that is robust, adaptable, and capable of providing stability and comfort in later years.

Here are a few strategies to address financial planning:

1. Understanding Retirement Accounts

Retirement accounts are vital for sustained financial planning, offering a range of options for varying necessities. In addition to choices like 401(k)s and IRAs, there are accounts specifically for self-employed individuals and small businesses, like SEP IRAs and SIMPLE IRAs. SEP IRAs allow contributions for those with incomes while SIMPLE IRAs are known for being user friendly and cost effective.

Understanding the nuances of employer match programs in 401(k) plans is crucial. Such programs can significantly boost your retirement savings, making it important to contribute enough to gain the full employer match. Additionally, the vesting schedule of your 401(k) plan, which determines when you gain full ownership of employer contributions, is a key aspect to understand.

For high earners, strategies like backdoor Roth IRA conversions offer a pathway to sidestep income limits and benefit from tax-free growth associated with Roth IRAs. These diverse types of retirement accounts, each with their own set of benefits and limitations, require careful consideration to optimize retirement savings effectively.

2. Strategies for Retirement Accounts

When developing strategies for retirement accounts, it's important to have an understanding of each account type. The timing of contributions plays a crucial role; making early contributions in the year can maximize investment growth while spreading out contributions throughout the year can take advantage of dollar cost averaging to mitigate the impact of market volatility.

Consolidating retirement accounts from employers can simplify overall management and possibly reduce associated fees, leading to a more streamlined investment strategy. One beneficial tactic is performing a Roth conversion. Moving funds from an IRA to a Roth IRA proves advantageous if you anticipate being in higher tax brackets during retirement. However, it's crucial to consider tax implications during the conversion year.

Understanding the sequence of withdrawals is also important for maintaining tax efficiency. Typically, this means withdrawing first from taxable accounts, then from tax-deferred accounts, and finally from Roth accounts. Consistently updating your strategy in reaction to modifications in tax legislation and retirement fund rules is imperative. Seeking guidance from financial consultants ensures your retirement approach stays pertinent, efficient, and in tune with the latest economic developments.

3. Investment Choices

The options available for retirement funds are diverse catering to risk preferences and financial goals. People often choose Exchange Traded Funds (ETFs), Real Estate Investment Trusts (REITs), and Certificates of Deposit (CDs) as traditional stocks, bonds and mutual funds. ETFs are particularly popular due to their management costs and wide market diversification.

REITs provide an accessible path into property investments, often with the benefit of appealing dividend yields, which can be a substantial income source during retirement. CDs, known for their safety as fixed-income investments, guaranteed returns, albeit typically at lower interest rates than other investments.

They are a reliable choice for those aiming to safeguard capital, particularly as retirement approaches.

These diverse investment options enable retirees to create portfolios that match their specific fiscal targets and risk attitudes. This personalization is crucial for attaining a balanced growth and income mix during retirement years, enhancing overall financial security and peace of mind.

4. Rebalancing and Diversification

A well-balanced and diversified investment portfolio is indispensable for effective risk management in investments. This approach entails diversifying investments across national and international markets, including stocks and bonds, to minimize the risks linked with any particular market. International investments, however, come with their own set of challenges, such as currency fluctuations and political uncertainties, which need to be carefully considered.

Rebalancing is a critical aspect of portfolio management, ensuring that the investment mix remains aligned with an individual's risk tolerance and financial goals. This involves modifying the distribution of various asset types in response to market shifts and personal economic changes. Automating this rebalancing process helps maintain focus on long-term goals and avoids emotional reactions to short-term market changes.

Regular reviews and modifications of the investment mix are essential, especially following significant life events or economic transformations. This ongoing process ensures the investment strategy remains suitable for the person's changing financial needs and goals.

5. Tax-Efficient Withdrawal Strategies

Developing tax-efficient withdrawal methods is crucial for maximizing retirement savings benefits. Strategically timing withdrawals from different account types, considering their varied tax implications, can significantly boost tax efficiency. For example, prioritizing withdrawals from taxable accounts before moving to tax-deferred accounts and then Roth accounts can optimize the tax burden.

Long-term capital gains, typically taxed at a lower rate than ordinary income, favor investments held for more than a year. Implementing Roth conversions during periods of lower income can lead to considerable tax savings, coupled with the advantage of tax-free withdrawals in later years. State tax laws also influence withdrawal strategies, as they vary in how retirement income is taxed.

Integrating charitable contributions, especially for those over 70½, into withdrawal plans can meet Required Minimum Distributions (RMDs) while reducing taxable income. Tailoring these strategies to individual situations and financial goals is key to extending retirement funds' longevity and efficacy, ensuring a more secure and comfortable retirement.

6. Longevity and Inflation Considerations

One significant concern in retirement planning is longevity risk—the possibility of outliving one's savings. Additionally, inflation continuously erodes purchasing power making it crucial to incorporate strategies that address both these factors. Inflation Protected Securities (IPS), like Treasury Inflation Protected Securities (TIPS), have been created to protect against inflation and ensure that retirement savings retain their worth over the term.

An annuity is another viable, which provides an income stream that can support you throughout your retirement thereby reducing the risk associated with longevity. When choosing annuities, it is crucial to evaluate the terms and conditions well as thoroughly comprehend the associated fees and potential outcomes. Additionally, keeping a portion of the investment portfolio in growth-focused assets, like stocks, helps counteract inflation effects. This requires a careful balance, as higher growth potential usually carries increased risk.

Regularly reviewing and adjusting withdrawal rates is also critical to ensure the sustainability of retirement funds. Strategies like the "4% rule" act as a starting point, but need to be customized to individual situations, market conditions, and physical health. These factors are crucial for creating a retirement plan that is robust, adaptable, and capable of adjusting to changing economic situations and personal life stages.

7. Seeking Professional Guidance

Steering through the intricacies of retirement planning often calls for expert advice. Financial advisors offer more than advice on investments; they aid in formulating extensive retirement plans that encompass a variety of elements such as estate planning, tax strategies, insurance needs, and income planning for retirement. Opting to engage with a Certified Financial Planner (CFP) or a Chartered Financial Analyst (CFA) hinges on personal requirements, with CFPs typically delivering a wider scope of fiscal structuring and CFAs concentrating more on scrutinizing investments and supervising asset portfolios.

For those searching for cost-effective options or with less complex economic situations, robo-financial advisors offer a feasible alternative. These digital platforms administrate asset portfolios through computational algorithms, rendering them apt for augmenting conventional fiscal counsel or as an independent solution. Frequent discussions with financial advisors are essential to guarantee that retirement plans remain aligned, adjusting to shifts in personal circumstances, market trends, and legislative updates.

Financial advisors also play a crucial role in estate planning. Working in collaboration with legal professionals, they help ensure that estate plans, including wills and trusts, are properly structured to reflect individual wishes and provide financial security for future generations. This comprehensive approach is vital in securing a financial legacy and ensuring peace of mind in retirement.

The strategies outlined encompass a broad range of financial considerations, from understanding and optimizing retirement accounts to selecting suitable investment options and devising tax-efficient withdrawal strategies. Addressing longevity and inflation considerations, coupled with seeking professional guidance, forms a comprehensive approach to retirement planning. Each step, from budgeting and healthcare planning to estate planning and investment management, contributes to building a secure and comfortable retirement.

The Role of Budgeting and Healthcare Planning Post-55

"A budget is more than just a series of numbers on a page; it embodies our values."

-Barack Obama

This statement holds for post-55 retirement, marking a phase when disciplined budgeting and comprehensive healthcare planning become keystones of financial sustainability and personal well-being.

In the years beyond 55, effective budgeting is not merely about maintaining a balance sheet; it's a critical tool for realizing retirement dreams and managing financial responsibilities. This stage often transitions from regular salary to fixed income sources such as pensions, social security, or retirement savings. Hence, budgeting requires a keen understanding of these income streams and their alignment with evolving lifestyle choices and expenses. It's about reassessing spending patterns – housing costs may decrease if mortgages are paid off, but spending on leisure and travel might increase. Budgeting during this period must also adapt to the changing family dynamics, such as supporting adult children or contributing to grandchildren's education.

Creating a solid emergency fund gains paramount importance. This fund is essential for unexpected life events and managing irregular expenses that come with age, like home modifications for accessibility. An emergency fund helps mitigate the financial impact of these expenditures without disrupting the planned monthly budget.

Healthcare planning, tangled with budgeting, takes on increased significance post-55. As healthcare needs escalate with age, so do the associated costs. Balancing Medicare, supplemental policies, and prescription plans requires thorough research and understanding. It's vital to comprehend the nuances of different insurance plans, their coverage specifics, and out-of-pocket costs. This knowledge allows for informed decisions that align with individual health requirements and financial capacities.

Establishing an emergency health fund is another critical aspect of healthcare planning. This fund addresses unexpected medical expenses, such as emergency procedures or treatments not covered by insurance. It provides a financial cushion, ensuring that healthcare emergencies do not become financial burdens.

Long-term care is another essential element of healthcare planning post-55. Long-term care insurance can be a prudent investment, but it requires careful consideration of the costs and benefits. It is crucial to understand the expenses associated with different types of long-term care (in-home, assisted living, nursing homes) and how they integrate into one's overall financial plan. Early planning in this area is advisable, as insurance premiums are generally lower when one is younger and healthier.

Legal and financial preparation for potential incapacity is integral to healthcare planning. This involves setting up advanced healthcare directives and living wills to honor one's healthcare preferences. A power of attorney for healthcare and finances can safeguard interests and ensure that critical decisions are in trusted hands should one become incapable of making them.

In addition to personal budgeting and healthcare planning, this phase often involves broader financial considerations such as estate planning. This includes wills, trusts, and beneficiary designations, ensuring one's economic legacy is distributed as intended. Estate planning also intersects with healthcare planning, as it can include instructions for end-of-life care and decisions.

Moreover, post-55 is a time to consider philanthropic goals. Many individuals wish to allocate a portion of their estate or income to charitable causes. This aspect can be woven into budgeting and estate planning, reflecting personal values and legacy aspirations.

The importance of seeking professional advice in budgeting and healthcare planning cannot be overstated. Financial advisors, estate planners, and healthcare consultants can provide valuable insights and guidance, tailoring strategies to individual circumstances. These professionals ensure that plans are robust and compliant with current laws and flexible enough to adapt to future changes.

Ensuring Financial Security and its Societal Impact

"Financial freedom is available to those who learn about it and work for it."

-Robert Kiyosaki

This statement captures the essence of financial security post-55, a period that demands personal fiscal prudence and has a profound impact on the broader fabric of society. Ensuring financial security during these later years is a diverse challenge, encompassing more than personal comfort and extending into societal welfare.

A significant shift marks the journey toward financial security post-55: moving from an earning phase to a period predominantly reliant on savings and fixed income sources such as pensions or retirement investments. This transition is critical and requires careful and strategic financial planning. Inadequate preparation for this phase can lead to many challenges, not only for the individuals directly affected but also for their families and the wider community.

One of the primary consequences of insufficient financial planning is the increased risk of dependency. Older adults may rely on family members or government assistance programs without adequate savings and financial resources. This dependency can place a substantial burden on younger generations and can strain public resources, which are often limited. It highlights the necessity of sound financial planning as a personal responsibility and a societal imperative.

Moreover, the lack of financial security can lead to delayed retirement, forcing individuals to continue working beyond their physical or mental capacity. This situation impacts their quality of life and can affect workforce dynamics, potentially limiting job opportunities for younger individuals entering the job market.

Personal financial stability post-55 also influences community engagement and societal contributions. Financially secure individuals are more likely to volunteer, donate to charities, and participate in community activities. Their involvement and experience can be invaluable assets to local communities, fostering a sense of unity and support. Conversely, those struggling financially may be unable to participate in such societal contributions, leading to a loss of valuable community resources and weakening social bonds.

Additionally, financial security enables individuals to invest in sustainable practices and support ethical businesses. This conscious spending and investment can drive positive societal change, encouraging firms to adopt more sustainable and ethical practices. In this way, personal financial stability post-55 can contribute to broader environmental and social sustainability.

The societal impact of financial planning also extends to the healthcare system. Individuals with adequate financial resources are more likely to seek timely medical care and invest in preventive health measures. This proactive approach can lead to better health outcomes and reduce the burden on healthcare systems, which often face challenges in meeting the needs of an aging population. On the other hand, those without sufficient financial means may delay seeking necessary medical care, potentially leading to more severe health issues that require intensive and costly interventions.

Furthermore, financial security allows for better end-of-life planning, including the ability to fund long-term care needs and make informed decisions about estate planning. This planning provides peace of mind for the individuals and their families. It ensures that their assets are distributed according to their wishes, potentially benefiting charitable causes and contributing to societal welfare.

Chapter 5: Loneliness and Social Isolation

"Loneliness is the ultimate poverty."

-Pauline Phillips

This quote perfectly encapsulates the intense emptiness that accompanies loneliness – the lack of connection that we experience. The absence of people does not define loneliness but the absence of meaningful connection. Likewise, social isolation refers to a physical state where an individual lacks a social network and has few social interactions. Together, these phenomena represent substantial challenges, particularly as they affect an increasing number of individuals worldwide.

Loneliness is a subjective feeling – a conscious, cognitive feeling of disconnection, of being unseen, of not mattering to others, regardless of how much social contact a person has. It's the discordance between what someone wishes their social relationships were and what the relationships they have. You can be in a crowded room and feel lonely if your interactions have no depth or meaning.

Social isolation, however, is a more objective, observable state. It can be measured by the number of contacts a person has and the frequency and nature of their social interactions. You might look at the size of a person's social network, participation in social activities, or access to others for social support. Unlike loneliness, one does not need to feel lonely to be socially isolated. You can have few social contacts and be content, just as you can have many and feel isolated.

Let's first grasp these concepts through a metaphor:

Understanding loneliness and social isolation is akin to exploring an immense, shadowed forest where each individual stands alone among the trees. Just as the forest is vast and interconnected, so too is the human need for meaningful relationships and social connectivity. Yet, within this expanse, one can feel utterly secluded, surrounded by trees that seem to whisper of connections lost or never formed. This metaphor exemplifies the essence of loneliness as a subjective experience, where, despite being in a crowded room—or a dense forest—one can feel an acute sense of isolation. The trees, towering and numerous, represent the potential for connection that somehow remains out of reach, emphasizing the internal nature of loneliness, a feeling not mitigated by mere physical proximity to others. In this vast forest, echoes of laughter and conversation might reach one's ears, yet the personal connection to these sounds is as intangible as the mist that hangs between the trees, further illustrating the isolating nature of loneliness despite apparent social abundance.

Similarly, social isolation can be likened to finding oneself on an island surrounded by a vast ocean. The ocean's waters, representing the barrier to social interaction, isolate the island from the rest of the world. This physical separation is measurable, much like how social isolation can be quantified by the lack of social contact. Yet, the experience of being on the island varies greatly depending on the individual. For some, the island may feel like a peaceful retreat, a contented separation from the bustling world beyond. For others, it's a place of involuntary exile, where the waters around them highlight the distance from connection and community. The island, with its clear boundaries defined by the endless water, stands as a stark representation of social isolation, where the physical distance from others is visible and measurable, unlike the nebulous boundaries of loneliness.

In both metaphors, the emotional sphere of loneliness and the physical metrics of social isolation converge to highlight the complex interrelation between our internal states and external circumstances. It also reveals the nuanced truth that loneliness and social isolation, while related, are two distinct social experiences, each with its own problems and implications for wellness. These metaphors are more than just a way of showing the differences (and similarities) between loneliness and isolation. Rather, these metaphors also underline how profoundly these states alter our sense of being human and connected in the world. By exploring loneliness in a shadowed forest and isolation on a remote island, we can gain deeper insight and empathy into the various forms and faces of these inescapable aspects of the human condition.

The Dangers of Loneliness and Social Isolation

Addressing the perils of loneliness and social isolation demands a deep dive into the intricate and multifarious effects these states can have on individuals — particularly in our increasingly disconnected modern society. Though the nuances of loneliness — a subjective feeling of being alone — and social isolation — an objective lack of social contacts — can differ, their effects overlap, creating a vast web of psychological, physical, and societal consequences that can drastically undercut an individual's quality of life.

Below are the detailed explorations of these consequences:

Psychological Impacts

The impact of loneliness and social isolation on our well-being is profound and wide-ranging. These experiences can increase the likelihood of developing health conditions, such as depression and anxiety, which are quite common. When we feel disconnected, unsupported, and misunderstood, it can create a spiral where loneliness worsens our health issues, which then intensifies our feelings of loneliness. Breaking this cycle without any intervention can be particularly challenging.

Moreover, loneliness and social isolation can contribute to increased levels of stress and anxiety. Without a support network in place, individuals facing difficulties have opportunities to share their experiences or find relief from stress. Over time, this can result in heightened states of chronic stress, known to be a factor in mental health problems.

Furthermore, feeling lonely and isolated can have an impact on an individual's ability to manage their emotions effectively. This can result in heightened irritability, mood swings, and difficulties in establishing or maintaining relationships, which further isolates them from others. In psychology, negative thoughts tend to be magnified, while positive interactions are downplayed. This distorted perception of reality makes reconnecting seem overwhelming or unattainable for those trapped in the cycle of loneliness. Furthermore, being alone can weaken a person's understanding of their identity, leading them to question their role and significance within society. Consequently, this can intensify feelings of insignificance and disconnection.

Physical Health Risks

The dangers of loneliness and social isolation extend beyond the mind to affect the body. Research has established a link between these states and various physical health problems. For instance, individuals who report feeling lonely or who are socially isolated exhibit a higher risk of heart disease. The stress associated with feeling disconnected can contribute to increased blood pressure and heart rate, both of which are risk factors for heart disease.

Moreover, being lonely or socially isolated can weaken our system. The stress caused by feeling isolated can suppress our function, making us more vulnerable to infections and diseases. Additionally, these states have been linked to inflammation, which plays a role in health issues like diseases, heart disease, and even cancer.

Besides the health effects mentioned earlier, loneliness and social isolation can disrupt sleep patterns. This goes beyond having trouble falling or staying asleep; it can mess with our body's natural sleep cycle. This disruption can result in insomnia or excessive daytime sleepiness, worsening health conditions. When a person experiences isolation, their body's stress response is triggered, which results in the release of cortisol. This hormone, when at levels, can cause various health problems such as weight gain, digestive issues, and an increased likelihood of developing chronic diseases like Type 2 diabetes. The physical manifestation that signals loneliness has even been misdiagnosed for other severe conditions, leading to overstated concerns for healthy individuals and people who may not get the support they need. Not having that social support can hurt in other ways, too, leading to a lack of healthy behaviors like regular exercise and eating a balanced diet, which can compound the risk of developing these severe health conditions.

Cognitive Decline and Dementia

The cognitive risks associated with loneliness and social isolation have been found to acutely exacerbate cognitive decline among the aging population and increase susceptibility to dementia, in particular. This can visibly impact memory, attention, and overall thinking skills. Without a brain boost from engaging social connections, a lack of stimulation can accelerate cognitive deficits. Furthermore, apart from the decline in the quality of life on a regular basis, this situation can also give rise to an environment that is susceptible to more neurodegenerative severe conditions like Alzheimer's disease. There is a belief that active social involvement plays a role in safeguarding brain health by stimulating adaptability and fortifying cognitive abilities against cognitive deterioration. Therefore, the absence of such interactions can hasten the progression of cognitive impairment, making social connections an essential component of mental health maintenance in older adulthood. Additionally, loneliness has been associated with an increased susceptibility to developing late-life depression. Interestingly, this is where too many complex factors can undermine cognitive function in older people.

Behavioral and Lifestyle Changes

Loneliness and social isolation can intensely shape individual behaviors and lifestyle choices, often contributing to adverse health outcomes. Desperate to fill a void left by an absence of social connection, individuals may increasingly seek solace in unhealthy coping mechanisms. Overindulging in digital devices, binge-watching the latest dramas, or other passive activities typically supplant physical activity and face-to-face interactions that promote well-being. Far from resolving an individual's perceived isolation, these behaviors only compound the experience while promoting sedentary behavior that can lead to obesity and related consequences.

The emotional burden of loneliness can also manifest in eating disorders, ranging from undereating due to a lack of motivation to prepare meals to overeat as an emotional comfort, further endangering physical health. Together, this cycle of poor health choices, fueled by experiences of loneliness and social isolation, may present a significant obstacle to seeking social interaction and, in turn, create a self-sustaining loop of isolation and declining health.

Moreover, the impact on sleep extends to the disruption of natural sleep cycles, contributing to perpetual fatigue that can dampen mood, decrease energy levels, and impair cognitive function. This disruption of sleep architecture exacerbates the challenges of managing daily stressors, making it more difficult to engage in healthy lifestyle choices and seek out social connections. The compound effect of disrupted sleep, poor dietary habits, and a sedentary lifestyle not only worsens existing health conditions but also paves the way for new health issues, emphasizing the link between social well-being and overall health.

Societal Impacts

The impact of loneliness and social isolation extends beyond individuals. It has consequences for society as a whole. These conditions can result in higher healthcare expenses because those who feel lonely or socially isolated are more prone to health problems that necessitate medical care. Additionally, the reduced productivity and increased absenteeism linked to the health outcomes of loneliness and social isolation can have economic effects.

The widespread problem of loneliness and social isolation has far-reaching consequences for society, including burdens such as increased healthcare expenses and reduced productivity. However, it also significantly impacts community dynamics. When loneliness rates are high, people tend to participate in community activities, weakening the essential social bonds that hold a society together. This decline in capital can lead to heightened distrust and a decreased sense of safety within communities, ultimately undermining harmony and cohesion. Moreover, when individuals become socially isolated, intergenerational connections suffer, disrupting the transmission of knowledge and values. This can create a gap that further divides communities. Furthermore, the pervasiveness of loneliness can worsen existing inequalities since those who are already at risk due to factors may have fewer opportunities for social engagement, perpetuating cycles of isolation and disadvantage.

In sum, the dangers of loneliness and social isolation are multifaceted — affecting psychological well-being, physical health, cognitive functioning, behavior, and societal well-being. These conditions are not merely personal issues; they also have sweeping societal and public health implications that warrant a collaborative response.

Rediscovering Connection at 55

At 55, a person often encounters distinct circumstances that can greatly affect their social well-being. This age is more than just a milestone; it signifies a period where personal and social life dynamics can shift substantially. Unlike stages of adulthood typically characterized by building a career and raising a family, the years around 55 usually bring a period of introspection and change. During this phase, people are encouraged to reflect on their accomplishments, reevaluate their goals, and consider possibilities for the future.

This stage in life can also underscore the resilience developed over the years, providing a foundation for traversing the complexities of social relationships in later years. By the time an individual reaches 55, they have amassed a range of experiences, equipping them with unique skills and perspectives. This is a period where the depth of existing relationships often becomes clearer, offering a more substantial source of companionship and support. This phase also promotes the development of self-compassion and understanding, essential qualities for connecting with others.

Furthermore, this stage in life can prompt a shift in how individuals view their involvement in the community. Contributing to the local or broader community might take on new importance. These activities help reinforce the community's social fabric, establishing a legacy of involvement and connection. A renewed sense of community engagement often creates a feeling of being valued and necessary.

In addition, health and wellness become crucial in shaping the social experiences of those around 55. Keeping good health is integral to maintaining an active and socially connected lifestyle. Focusing on health is essential for ensuring the ability to participate in various activities and promoting mental clarity and emotional stability.

At 55, there is an opportunity for rediscovery. It's a period when individuals can explore new dimensions of social engagement, enriched by the wisdom that comes with age. This period is about more than just forming new connections; it's also about enhancing the quality of existing relationships and exploring unique aspects of oneself.

Strategies for Overcoming Loneliness and Social Isolation at 55: A Practical Guide

Despite the challenges of feelings of loneliness and social isolation, there are numerous strategies that one can employ to foster connections, enhance well-being, and counter these feelings effectively. The guide below aims to explore practical steps individuals can take to overcome loneliness and build a fulfilling social life at 55 and beyond.

Cultivating New Interests and Hobbies

Exploring new interests at 55 opens possibilities for personal growth and social connection. For example, taking up birdwatching or nature photography can lead you to join local or online communities with similar environmental interests. These hobbies provide a reason to venture outdoors, appreciate the natural world, and connect with others who share your enthusiasm for conservation and natural beauty. Furthermore, engaging in creative writing or joining a writers' group can offer a sense of companionship and mutual inspiration as you share stories, feedback, and encouragement. Each new hobby invites you into a community of peers, expanding your social network through shared passions and activities.

Leveraging Technology for Connection

The digital age makes staying connected more accessible than ever before. At 55, embracing social media platforms to share your life's milestones or everyday moments can rekindle old friendships and spark new ones. Participating in online forums dedicated to your hobbies or interests can also lead to meaningful connections with people worldwide. For those interested in lifelong learning, enrolling in online courses on history, science, or art allows you to engage with fellow learners and instructors, fostering a virtual community of curious minds. Technology, thus, acts as a bridge to overcoming physical distances, bringing like-minded individuals together in pursuit of common goals and interests.

Volunteering and Community Engagement

Giving back to the community through volunteering at 55 enriches the lives of others and your own. Engaging in activities such as tutoring students, working with animal rescue organizations, or participating in community beautification projects can offer new perspectives and deep satisfaction. These acts of service connect you with people across different age groups and walks of life, enriching your social life with diverse interactions and friendships. Moreover, leadership in organizing community events or fundraisers can position you as a key figure in your community, enhancing your social visibility and networks.

Strengthening Existing Relationships

At 55, nurturing existing relationships becomes more crucial than ever. Scheduling regular catch-ups with friends over coffee or dinner helps strengthen the bond, ensuring that friendships evolve alongside life's changes. Initiating group vacations or retreats with family members or close friends can create shared memories and experiences, reinforcing bonds and providing comfort and support. Additionally, engaging in mutual interest activities, like joining a dance class or a bowling league together, can introduce a new dimension to your relationships, keeping them vibrant and fulfilling.

Seeking Professional Support

Professional support at 55 can be a vital resource in managing loneliness. Engaging with a counselor specializing in adult life transitions can provide strategies for adjusting to changes and making new connections. Attending seminars or group therapy sessions focused on building social networks can offer practical advice and the opportunity to meet others facing similar challenges. Furthermore, joining a wellness group that focuses on holistic health practices can improve your physical well-being and social life as you meet others committed to maintaining their health and vitality.

Fostering a Positive Mindset

A positive mindset at 55 can influence social interactions and openness to new experiences. Practicing gratitude by acknowledging the good in your life can attract positivity and like-minded people. Engaging in volunteer work or acts of kindness benefits others and boosts your mood and outlook on life, making you more approachable and likely to form connections. Adopting a learning mindset toward technology and new social norms can also ease making new friends, allowing you to navigate social platforms and modern communication methods confidently.

Overcoming loneliness and social isolation at 55 requires a proactive, multi-layered approach, focusing on expanding your horizons, embracing technology, contributing to your community, deepening personal relationships, seeking support when needed, and maintaining a positive outlook on life. By actively pursuing these strategies, you can build a rich, fulfilling social life that not only counters feelings of loneliness but also adds depth and joy to your years beyond 55.

Overcoming Isolation: Lessons from 'To Kill a Mockingbird' on Connecting Deeply

A valuable insight into the theme of solitude and its significant effects, as exemplified by Pauline Phillips' observation, is presented in Harper Lee's *"To Kill a Mockingbird."* The character Boo Radley acts as a focal point for examining the deep impact of isolation and the essence of personal connections. Misinterpreted and avoided by the local community, Boo leads a secluded existence, becoming an enigma wrapped in rumor. Yet, as the tale progresses, it becomes evident that Boo's motives stem from a place of benevolence, challenging the assumption that physical distance is synonymous with emotional disconnection.

This story highlights the critical need to see past initial impressions to grasp the true nature of human bonds. It suggests that feelings of being alone can often emerge from being ostracized and that kindness and effort to comprehend others can close significant separation gaps. Boo Radley's narrative serves as proof that genuine interactions can emerge in the least expected settings, contesting the view that solitude is a definitive state.

This insight holds particular importance for addressing the solitude and social withdrawal individuals might face as they advance in age. It promotes a shift in how we view our connections and advocates for an active effort to establish substantial ties, underscoring the belief that initiating and nurturing relationships is always possible. Boo Radley's evolution from an object of dread to a symbol of warmth and connection demonstrates the incredible influence of empathy and understanding in surmounting the challenges of solitude and detachment.

Additionally, the narrative of *"Frankenstein"* by Mary Shelley provides another exploration of loneliness and the desperate yearning for connection. The creature, created and then abandoned by Victor Frankenstein, embodies the acute pain of isolation, marked not by his monstrous appearance but by his exclusion from human companionship. His initial innocence and desire for love and acceptance contrast with the fear and rejection he meets from every human he encounters.

Shelley's novel digs into the creature's profound loneliness, showing how exclusion and misunderstanding drive him to despair and vengeance. It accentuates a poignant lesson: the deep psychological impact of isolation can lead to destructive outcomes, both for the individual and society. The creature's attempts to communicate and connect, met with horror and violence, highlight the tragic consequences of failing to look beyond physical appearance and societal prejudices to the inherent need for companionship that exists within all beings.

"Frankenstein" complements the lessons drawn from "To Kill a Mockingbird" by emphasizing that isolation is not just a physical state but an emotional and psychological experience that deeply affects one's actions and interactions. Both Boo Radley and the creature in "Frankenstein" show that empathy, understanding, and the effort to connect can bridge the vastest divides. Shelley's narrative, like Lee's, calls for reevaluating the biases and fears that keep us from extending compassion and understanding to those who appear different or distant.

Together, these stories reinforce the idea that overcoming isolation requires more than just the physical presence of others; it necessitates a willingness to engage with and understand the inherent worth and desires for connection within everyone. They teach us that through empathy and the courage to confront our prejudices, we can dismantle the barriers of loneliness and forge meaningful relationships, even under the most unlikely circumstances.

Regrets and Unfulfilled Dreams at 55

Reaching the age of 55 brings a period of introspection, where the reflections on past decisions, roads not taken, and dreams left on the shelf become more pronounced. This stage of life often prompts individuals to look back on their years, assessing the outcomes of their choices and confronting the realities of unfulfilled ambitions. The essence of this contemplation can lead to an understanding of one's life narrative, characterized by achievements and areas left unexplored.

One common regret among those at this stage is the career paths not pursued, or the professional opportunities missed due to fear, indecision, or circumstances.

Consider the example of Michael, a 55-year-old accountant associated with a large firm in the city. For years, Michael had nurtured a passion for landscape photography, a hobby that allowed him to capture the beauty of the natural world through his lens. His talent was evident; on several occasions, friends and family encouraged him to pursue this passion professionally. They saw in his photographs a rare gift, a way of seeing the world that could surely find a broader audience. Yet, Michael always considered photography a secondary pursuit, a leisure activity for weekends and vacations, not something to base a career on.

Years ago, Michael had stumbled upon an opportunity that might have altered the course of his professional life. A well-known nature magazine was searching for a new photographer to join their team, an opportunity that seemed tailor-made for Michael. It would have meant leaving the security of his accounting job, relocating to a different city, and stepping into the uncertain world of freelance photography. The thought thrilled him; it was a dream job, aligning perfectly with his passion and skills. However, the risks involved—the uncertainty of a steady income, the fear of failing in a highly competitive field, and the daunting prospect of starting over in a new city—held him back. He decided against applying, telling himself that his current career, though less fulfilling, offered stability and security.

Now, at 55, Michael often finds himself reflecting on that decision. As he sits in his office, surrounded by spreadsheets and financial reports, he can't help but wonder about the path not taken. He imagines the adventures he could have had, traveling to exotic locations, capturing the world's wonders through his camera, and sharing his vision with others. The regret is intense, a sense of loss not just for the job he didn't pursue but for the part of himself that remained unexpressed. Michael realizes that the decision made out of fear and a desire for security has cost him more than just a career change; it has meant sidelining his true passion and, perhaps, a part of his identity.

This reflection on missed opportunities and unfulfilled potential is not unique to Michael. Many find themselves pondering the "what ifs" of career decisions, contemplating how different life might have been had they taken that job offer in a different city or pursued their passion instead of a more secure but less fulfilling job. This reflection is often tinged with a sense of loss for the professional identity that could have been, alongside a realization of the fleeting nature of career opportunities.

Another significant area of reflection is personal relationships, particularly those that have frayed or dissolved over time. The value of deep, meaningful connections becomes harshly apparent, leading to regret over neglected friendships or family ties strained beyond repair. The busy nature of life's earlier years, with its focus on career and raising a family, sometimes means that relationships were not given the attention they deserved. Looking back, the importance of these bonds becomes painfully clear, as does the difficulty of rekindling connections that have weakened or vanished.

For many, unfulfilled dreams and aspirations also represent a source of regret. These dreams are set aside in the face of practical considerations or postponed in pursuing obligations and responsibilities. Whether it's the book never written, the business never started, or the adventure never taken, these unfulfilled dreams linger as reminders of what might have been. The awareness that time is becoming more precious can exacerbate the sense of missed opportunities and the longing for what was once possible.

Financial decisions, too, come under scrutiny. The impact of earlier financial choices becomes evident as individuals assess their readiness for retirement and consider the legacy they wish to leave. Regrets may surface over not saving enough, malinvesting, or not planning adequately for the future. These financial reflections are often accompanied by concerns about the stability and security of one's later years and the desire to provide for loved ones.

Take the case of Alex, who, at 55, looks back with regret at his approach to financial planning. In his younger years, Alex enjoyed the thrill of the stock market, often investing in high-risk ventures without much thought for the long term. While some investments paid off, many did not, leaving him with a sense of what could have been had he opted for a more balanced and cautious strategy.

As he reviews his retirement accounts and thinks about the future he wishes to secure for his family, the realization hits him hard. The dream of a comfortable retirement and the ability to support his children's aspirations seems distant, a direct consequence of earlier financial gambles that didn't pan out.

For many at 55, the realization that neglecting physical exercise, succumbing to unhealthy eating patterns, or overlooking mental health has led to current health challenges brings a sense of regret. This hindsight stresses the critical balance between caring for oneself and meeting life's demands, a balance often skewed in youth. The clash between the aspiration for active, vibrant later years and the reality of physical constraints reflects the long-term impact of earlier wellness choices, marking a significant area of reflection and regret.

The societal and cultural contributions one hoped to make can also be a source of regret. Many at 55 reflect on whether they have made a meaningful impact on the world around them, whether through community involvement, advocacy, or creative expression. There's a contemplation of the difference one has made, or perhaps the lack thereof, leading to questions about legacy and the mark one leaves on society.

Imagine life's societal and cultural contributions as seeds planted in a vast garden. At 55, many stand at the edge of this garden, surveying the growth and blooms that have sprung from the seeds they've sown over the years. Some garden areas are lush and vibrant, showcasing the positive impacts of community involvement, advocacy, and creative expression. Yet, there are also patches left barren or neglected, where seeds were never planted due to hesitation, fear, or missed opportunities. This garden becomes a metaphor for the legacy one hopes to leave behind, with each plant contributing to the world's social and cultural fabric. The contemplation of this garden brings to light the areas of untapped potential, sparking reflection on the marks left unmade and the contributions that could have enriched the garden further, adding to its diversity and beauty.

Amid these reflections, a quote by American author John Green echoes deeply: *"It's so hard to leave—until you leave. And then it's the easiest thing in the world."* This sentiment carries the essence of regret—realizing that the barriers to pursuing dreams or making different choices were often not as insurmountable as they seemed. Looking back, the possibilities for a different path or a life more aligned with one's aspirations can seem both tantalizingly close and frustratingly out of reach.

In the midlife stage, the contrasts between achievements and unmet goals, between the paths taken and those left unexplored, come into sharp relief. The reflections on unfulfilled dreams and regrets at 55 are an influential reminder of the complexity of life's journey. They underline the importance of choices made and the impact of those choices on the narrative of one's life. This period of reflection, while challenging, also offers an opportunity for acceptance and understanding, providing a foundation for moving forward with grace and wisdom.

Turning Regrets and Unfulfilled Dreams at 55

This guide provides a road map for those standing at this critical crossroads of regrets and unfulfilled dreams at 55, aiming to transform reflections of what might have been into actionable steps toward a future filled with purpose and fulfillment.

Below are the strategies to address these feelings, providing a structured approach to transforming these reflections into a positive force for change and fulfillment in life.

Acknowledging and Learning from Regrets

Acknowledging regrets involves a candid look back at decisions made and opportunities missed, understanding that these past experiences are integral to one's personal growth. It's about accepting these moments without judgment, recognizing them as pivotal steps in life's journey. This acceptance allows individuals to extract valuable lessons from their past, providing a clearer perspective on what truly matters. By learning from regrets, one can identify patterns in decision-making, understand the consequences of certain choices, and use this knowledge to inform future actions. This process of reflection and learning is essential for moving forward, turning regrets into valuable insights that pave the way for growth and positive change.

Identifying and Refining Unfulfilled Dreams

At 55, revisiting unfulfilled dreams offers an opportunity to reassess which aspirations still hold personal significance. This involves differentiating between dreams that continue to inspire passion and those that no longer align with one's current values or life situation. By identifying and refining these dreams, individuals can focus on goals that truly resonate with their authentic selves. This step requires introspection and honesty, as it is crucial to acknowledge that some dreams may have evolved or changed over time. Refining unfulfilled dreams in this way ensures that future pursuits are significant and reflective of one's current aspirations, setting a foundation for a fulfilling path ahead.

Charting a Course Forward

With refined goals, charting a course forward involves careful planning and setting achievable milestones. This phase is about translating dreams into actionable plans, detailing the steps necessary to achieve these aspirations. Establishing a straightforward, structured approach provides a road map for action, breaking down larger goals into smaller, manageable tasks. This actionable plan should include timelines, resources needed, potential obstacles, and strategies for overcoming them. Regular review and adjustment of the plan ensure it remains aligned with one's evolving goals and circumstances, keeping the journey toward fulfillment on track.

Building a Supportive Network

Cultivating a supportive network is crucial for facing the challenges of pursuing unfulfilled dreams. This network, composed of friends, family, and like-minded individuals, offers emotional support, encouragement, and practical advice. Sharing one's aspirations and progress with a supportive community can bolster motivation and resilience, providing a sense of accountability and belonging. Additionally, this network can serve as a valuable resource for diverse perspectives and experiences, offering guidance and insight to inform one's journey. Building and nurturing these relationships create a foundation of support that can make pursuing dreams a shared and enriching experience.

Embracing Adaptability and Continuous Growth

Embracing adaptability means being open to change and willing to modify one's path as new information and opportunities emerge. This flexibility allows individuals to gracefully traverse the uncertainties of pursuing unfulfilled dreams, adjusting their strategies in response to life's inevitable shifts. Coupled with a commitment to continuous growth, adaptability ensures that one's approach to fulfilling dreams remains dynamic and responsive. This mindset encourages lifelong learning, exploring new possibilities, and the resilience to face setbacks. By fostering adaptability and a dedication to growth, individuals can pursue their aspirations with curiosity and openness, ready to embrace the journey's twists and turns.

Finding Fulfillment in the Present

While pursuing unfulfilled dreams is forward-looking, finding fulfillment in the present moment is vital. This involves appreciating the journey toward one's goals, celebrating small successes, and practicing gratitude for the opportunities and experiences of chasing dreams. Emphasizing present fulfillment encourages a mindful approach to life, where joy is not solely contingent on future achievements but is found in striving toward them. This perspective fosters a balanced approach to life, where pursuing dreams enhances one's daily experiences, contributing to a profound sense of contentment and well-being. Eckhart Tolle wisely stated, *'Acknowledging the good that you already have in your life is the foundation for all abundance.'* This quote represents the importance of recognizing and valuing the present as a key component of a fulfilling journey, regardless of the destination.

As we step into life's next chapter, we discover that the true measure of success is the depth of our experiences, the insights we've gathered, and the happiness we find in following our passions. At 55, the adventure is far from concluding; it is entering a phase filled with potential and awaiting discoveries.

Chapter 6: Family and Relationships

"How can we maintain strong family bonds as we enter our later years?" This question is crucial as individuals reach the phase beyond 55, embarking on a journey filled with transformation and adjustments within their family structures. This time, often viewed as an era of relaxation and fulfillment, presents unique challenges and shifts that can profoundly affect family dynamics. This chapter explores the nuances of relationships during this significant life stage, stressing the importance of deep understanding and adaptation to sustain harmony and connection among family members.

As individuals age, the foundation of family relationships experiences a major shift. The once familiar roles evolve, leading to a reevaluation of how these changes affect both personal identity and family interactions. When parents become grandparents, they experience a shift in their daily roles and how they interact with their family on an emotional and social level. This repositioning can lead to emotions of contentment and happiness, but it can also cause loss and doubt about one's prior place in the family structure.

This period is often accompanied by the loss of peers, friends, and family members, which introduces a layer of grief and adjustment into the family dynamics. The loss experience necessitates reconfiguring emotional ties and support networks within the family, posing a challenge to maintaining the usual flow of interactions and emotional support. Each member's process of coping with grief can affect others, sometimes bringing people closer together while, at other times, creating distances that were not there before.

In addition to these shifts, the way families communicate undergoes significant changes. As adult children start their own families, occupations, and lifestyles, finding common ground for meaningful interactions can be difficult. This is made more difficult by the quick development of technology as the primary form of communication, which could make senior family members feel excluded or alone. On the other hand, younger family members can find it difficult to relate to their elders' experiences and points of view, which could cause a sense of detachment between them.

Maintaining the strength of the family unit requires adjusting to new communication methods. This adaptation goes beyond merely keeping up with the latest digital communication tools; it fosters an environment where every member feels valued and heard, ensuring regular and meaningful exchanges and bridging generational divides. This mutual effort can strengthen family ties, making the later years of life a rich, intergenerational connection rather than isolation.

By proactively addressing these challenges, families can traverse the changes brought on by aging, transforming potential obstacles into opportunities for growth and deeper connection. Open conversations about evolving roles, an empathetic approach to loss and grief, and a commitment to bridging communication gaps can fortify family bonds, ensuring that the later years are enriched with support, understanding, and mutual respect.

Understanding Changing Family Dynamics

As individuals step into the phase beyond 55, a profound transformation unfolds within the structure of family dynamics. This era, often paralleled with milestones such as retirement and the advent of the empty nest phase, prompts a profound reassessment of one's identity and the intricacies of parental and grandparental relationships. This juncture in life is not merely about transitioning roles but redefining the essence of these connections in the face of evolving needs and expectations.

The pivot from being the primary caretaker to a figure of support and guidance condenses a significant adjustment for many parents. This evolution demands a dance between offering wisdom and respecting the burgeoning independence of their adult offspring. The inherent challenge lies in suppressing the instinct to direct, favoring a support stance, and being ready to impart wisdom when sought. This recalibration can be disorienting, necessitating a shift in parental self-perception and acknowledging their evolving contribution to their children's lives.

Grandparenthood introduces a further dimension to this transitional phase. The role of the modern grandparents has become more complex and significant due to geographical dispersion, extended longevity, and the intricacy of modern family arrangements. Grandparents can play a crucial role in the upbringing of their grandchildren by acting as dependable emotional pillars or by offering vital childcare support. Yet, this heightened involvement beckons a nuanced approach to navigating the delicate line of respecting their adult children's autonomy in parenting. Effective, open communication becomes the cornerstone of harmonizing these expanded roles, ensuring that support is provided without encroaching upon the established boundaries of the nuclear family unit.

Simultaneously, this period heralds a mutual adaptation process wherein adult children begin to perceive their parents through a new lens. Parents transition from authority figures to esteemed advisors, and their life experiences and wisdom gain newfound recognition and value. This development could strengthen the link between parents and children and provide the groundwork for a future in which respect and understanding are mutually reinforcing. However, as both parties negotiate the subtleties of these rearranged roles and boundaries, it presents a complicated array of emotional issues.

Coping with Loss and Grief

As we grow older, it is inevitable to experience loss and grief. This is a time for restructuring the emotions and relationships within the family unit. Peers, siblings, and sometimes even one's children moving out causes a significant upheaval in the family environment, requiring changes to roles, support systems, and communication patterns.

These losses affect the family's dynamics and the immediate emotional toll. This instance highlights how important it is to have open, honest communication and create safe spaces where people may disclose their weaknesses without worrying about judgment. A robust support system is necessary, acknowledging each person's grief process's individuality while promoting a collective recovery journey.

Furthermore, dealing with loss frequently forces family members to carefully reevaluate their priorities, pushing them to develop closer ties and leave a legacy that pays tribute to the deceased. This can take many forms, such as creating new family customs, honoring the deceased, or a stronger focus on spending quality time together and ensuring that every moment is filled with love and importance.

The process of coping with loss and grieving also reveals the resiliency and strength of familial ties, emphasizing how these connections may change and grow even amid extreme sadness. It is evidence of the continuing power of family love, which can overcome the sorrow of bereavement and rekindle a feeling of purpose and unity.

When dealing with loss and sadness, families are reminded of how short life can be and how precious it is to spend time with loved ones. It's a time when people reflect, grow, and develop an understanding of the relationships that make up their family. By supporting each other, having conversations, and honoring the memories of those who have passed away, families can navigate the difficult times of grief. In doing so, they emerge with bonds and a renewed dedication to cherishing every moment together.

A specific practice to support this process is the establishment of a 'Memory Garden' within the family home or community. This garden serves as a living tribute to the loved ones lost, where family members can plant flowers, trees, or shrubs that remind them of the deceased. Each plant can be accompanied by a small plaque or stone engraved with the loved one's name, allowing family members to remember and honor them tangibly. Caring for the garden becomes a therapeutic activity, providing a space for reflection, healing, and connection with nature. This practice fosters a sense of continuity and legacy. It encourages the family to gather and share stories and memories, reinforcing the bonds between them as they traverse their grief together.

Adapting to New Communication Patterns

Families now communicate differently, reflecting the digital age, which has broken down barriers and created previously unheard-of chances for connection. Although this change has many positive aspects, it also brings distinct difficulties, especially for people over 55. Both older and younger family members must ensure that technology promotes inclusivity and strengthens rather than divides family ties as the digital divide closes.

For seniors, the rapid pace of technological advancement can be daunting. Social media platforms, video calls, and instant messaging represent more than new communication methods; they embody a shift in relationships and interactions. Adopting these technologies necessitates mastering the subtleties of digital communication and picking up new skills like device and program usage. For example, it can be difficult to decipher tone and intent when no visual indicators are present, and people used to more conventional modes of communication may find the transient nature of digital interactions less significant. Finding a balance and setting a comfortable pace for using technology is essential since seniors may become overwhelmed and exhausted due to the continual updates across several platforms and the abundance of information available. This issue emphasizes the necessity of a deliberate approach to seniors' technology integration, ensuring that technology improves rather than complicates their relationships with others.

Yet, there are a lot of advantages to learning these new skills. Family members who are physically separated can still come together for shared experiences due to digital communication, which can span great distances. From first steps to graduation ceremonies, grandparents may watch life milestones in real-time with their grandkids, providing a sense of presence and participation that was not previously conceivable. Likewise, adult offspring can provide assistance and consistent communication to their aging parents, guaranteeing that familial ties endure even when in-person visits are restricted due to life's obligations.

However, younger family members are essential in helping this shift, so elderly members are not the only ones who need to adjust. This calls for more than simply troubleshooting problems and technological help; it also calls for patience and a readiness to comprehend the emotional and psychological challenges that their seniors may encounter. In this setting, education becomes a two-way street where younger people learn from their elder relatives' preferences, worries, and experiences while sharing their digital insights.

A family culture that embraces and makes good use of digital communication, such as that provided by "FamilyApp," can help reduce the risk of isolation in older persons. Furthermore, it's critical to understand that digital communication should complement face-to-face interactions rather than replace them. These resources and customary in-person meetings and phone conversations can build a complex web of interaction that promotes each family member's emotional health.

Real-Life Example

To illustrate these dynamics, consider the story of the Nguyen family. In their late 60s, the parents faced the challenge of supporting their adult children through significant life changes while balancing their transition into retirement. At the same time, they were adapting to their role as grandparents, striving to support their children's parenting choices while forming meaningful bonds with their grandchildren.

When Mr. Nguyen faced a health scare, the family had to confront the reality of caregiving and the potential need for long-term care options. These conversations exposed varying viewpoints among family members. However, the family managed to tackle this problematic circumstance by having an honest discussion and being dedicated to coming up with a solution that respected Mr. Nguyen's wishes.

Tips and Tricks for Better Family Relationships

Below are the fundamental pillars for nurturing strong family relationships: investing quality time, establishing and respecting boundaries, managing conflicts constructively, and sharing responsibilities. These practices form the foundation stone of a supportive and harmonious family environment.

This guide delves into practical strategies to enhance family dynamics, promote unity, and cultivate belonging among all members. By prioritizing these essential elements, families can create lasting bonds that weather life's challenges and celebrate its joys.

1.   Invest in Quality Time

Investing one's time together as a family is crucial for maintaining and strengthening those bonds that unite them. Regularly scheduled activities or outings allow family members to commune, share experiences, and create lasting recollections. Whether it be a routine shared repast, a weekend escapade into the wilderness, or participating in a joint hobby, these instants are priceless. They provide a break from the routine and enable family members to appreciate each other's presence significantly. Spending quality moments together fosters unity and affection, reinforcing the household's base and enhancing its strength amid ordeals. Weekly game nights and spontaneous day trips deepen comprehension as varied conversations flow. A family that plays together thrives together, as memories cement their cohesion through any adversity.

2 Establish and Respect Boundaries

Acknowledging each other's boundaries is essential to fostering mutual respect in any family. Personal space, privacy, and independence are important boundaries that shape our relationships. Through clear communication about these boundaries, misunderstandings can be avoided and a healthy balance found. Respecting boundaries acknowledges that family is important but that individual lives, with varied choices and responsibilities, also deserve respect. When each member's needs and preferences are considered, personal growth is supported alongside the collective well-being of the family unit. Respecting boundaries allows the family bond to thrive while nurturing independence.

3 Manage Conflicts Constructively

Resolving disputes productively is crucial to keeping the family united. It entails approaching conflicts by emphasizing coming to a mutually beneficial solution more than placing blame. This approach strengthens and joins the family by creating an atmosphere where all members feel valued and heard. Strategies for resolving conflicts that work include compromise, attentive listening, and clear communication. For example, family members might explore different choices and consider each other's goals and restrictions when there is a disagreement about vacation plans rather than imposing their preferences. This cooperative method not only settles the present problem but also establishes a good example for resolving problems in the future, ensuring that disagreements become chances for growth rather than causes for division.

4 Share Responsibilities

It is essential to foster a spirit of teamwork within the family by assigning tasks to one another. By allocating responsibilities fairly, this strategy ensures that each member's workload is recognized and manageable. For instance, dividing home chores according to interest, skill, and age can make the process less stressful and more effective for all parties. Acknowledging and valuing the contributions of each individual promotes a sense of community and group success. A method like this strengthens the bonds within the family by encouraging cooperation and responsibility while also assisting in the smooth administration of the household. To illustrate, let's consider the Johnson family, where each weekend, they gather to decide the coming week's chores. Tom, the father, enjoys gardening and cares for the lawn and garden. Marie, the mother and cooking enthusiast, handles meal planning and grocery shopping. Their teenage son, Alex, tech-savvy and robust, is responsible for technology updates and carrying heavy groceries. Lastly, their daughter, Emma, who loves organizing, takes on decluttering and organizing the living spaces. This approach ensures that tasks are completed efficiently and allows each family member to engage in activities they find fulfilling, enhancing their overall happiness and unity.

5 Support Each Other's Wellness

Supporting the family's collective health, covering both physical and emotional aspects, is vital for its comprehensive well-being. Motivating consistent physical activity, nutritious eating habits, and ample rest enhances everyone's physical condition. Likewise, giving attention to and addressing each other's psychological health requirements is essential. This includes supporting one another emotionally during trying times and advocating for professional assistance when needed. For example, organizing family walks or enrolling in group exercise programs can have positive psychological and physical effects. This collective approach to wellness highlights the value of health and shows a dedication to one another's welfare.

6 Listen Actively

Beyond merely processing spoken words, active listening involves fully immersing oneself in the speaker to grasp their intended message and feelings. This requires giving undivided attention, establishing eye contact, and providing feedback that shows you grasp their perspective. When a family member shares about their day, for example, set aside your devices and listen with the intention of understanding rather than merely answering. Show your sincere interest in learning more about their experiences by asking follow-up questions or making remarks. By validating their emotions, active listening helps them feel important and fortifies the relationship within the family. It elevates simple discussions into deep dialogues that strengthen ties and foster trust within the family.

7 Offer Unconditional Support

Being there for family members during both celebrations and challenges, free from criticism or limitations, embodies the essence of providing unconditional support. Regardless of the circumstances, the assurance that one is never isolated instills strength and reassurance. Such support acts as a protective buffer. For instance, if a family member experiences a financial loss, such as a significant investment downturn on a platform like Binance, or undergoes a personal hurdle, extending unwavering encouragement, compassion, and tangible aid can markedly affect their ability to bounce back. Offering this level of support cultivates resilience and promotes a sense of security, reinforcing the family as a bastion of constant love and acceptance.

8 Foster Independence

To foster independence in the family, one must support one another's goals, passions, and choices while acknowledging the need for personal development and autonomy for overall well-being. This support can take many forms, such as supporting a family member's desire to relocate overseas for employment or school or encouraging kids to follow their hobbies even if they deviate from family customs. Assuring that the family continues to be a reliable source of support and encouragement while simultaneously giving the child the skills and self-assurance necessary to explore and manage the outside world is part of fostering independence. A specific strategy to enhance this practice is the introduction of 'Independence Projects' for each family member. This involves setting aside time for individuals to work on a personal project or goal that is meaningful to them. At the same time, the rest of the family provides support, resources, or feedback as needed. For instance, a teenager interested in coding could be given time and space to develop their own app, with family members testing it and offering constructive criticism. This approach validates the individual's interests and autonomy and integrates their pursuits into the fabric of family life, fostering a sense of independence within a supportive community framework.

9 Prioritize Forgiveness

Setting forgiveness as a top priority is crucial to recovering from disagreements and misunderstandings and moving on. Grievances that are held onto might cause enduring divisions in the family. On the other hand, forgiveness promotes growth and reconciliation. To be forgiven is to choose to let go of hatred for the sake of the family as a whole, not to forget or justify painful behavior. For instance, turning a potentially polarizing situation into a chance to build trust can be achieved by forgiving and having an open mind while addressing a mistake. Families can continue caring and helpful even in difficult times if they value forgiveness.

10 Establish Routine Check-Ins

Regular family check-ins or meetings are essential to preserving good communication and resolving conflicts. During these meetings, members have a specific time to voice their ideas, emotions, and worries in a secure and encouraging setting. Families may ensure that each person feels heard and has a voice by creating a routine for these talks. It also identifies any underlying issues or tensions that may need to be addressed, preventing them from escalating into more significant conflicts. Additionally, routine check-ins help to strengthen familial bonds by fostering a sense of unity and collaboration. Family members can work to overcome obstacles and recognize successes, fostering a caring environment where everyone feels substantial and respected.

11 Create Family Traditions

Family traditions play a vital role in strengthening bonds and creating lasting memories. Whether it's a weekly game night, a monthly movie marathon, or an annual holiday celebration, these rituals provide families with opportunities to connect. Traditions offer stability and continuity amidst life's changes, grounding family members in their shared experiences and values. They also reinforce the maintenance of family identity and foster pride and belonging. Engaging in traditions promotes emotions of intimacy and unity since family members engage in the pleasures and problems of these unique occasions. Family relationships can be strengthened, and a solid foundation of love and support can be established by establishing and upholding significant traditions.

12 Encourage Individual Growth

To promote a positive family dynamic, supporting personal growth and development is imperative. Encouragement of each family member to follow their hobbies, interests, and objectives fosters self-expression and autonomy. Families should support and encourage their children at every stage, whether seeking professional prospects, learning new hobbies, or expanding their education. For instance, Sarah's family supported her emerging interest in photography by getting her a camera and signing her up for a class when she mentioned her interest in the subject. Michael's family supported him throughout his studies and celebrated his acceptance when he decided to return to school for his Master's degree, highlighting education as a treasured family endeavor. Families foster an environment of optimism and empowerment by acknowledging and applauding one another's accomplishments. Family members supported in personal development are also more resilient, self-assured, and purposeful. A more prosperous, more satisfying existence for the whole family results from each member thriving and realizing their full potential.

13 Practice Gratitude

Gratitude is a potent tool for building family bonds and creating a happy environment at home. Encouraging family members to acknowledge each other's contributions cultivates appreciation, and genuinely recognizing one's efforts, no matter how small, fosters an enduring sense of value. Members feel validated in their roles through thoughtful recognition of their kindness and support and feel heard on a deeper level. Moreover, the heartfelt expressions of gratitude shift one's perspective outward, promoting sensitivity to the needs and emotions of others profoundly. As compassion circulates through the family dynamic, negativity and discord recede, allowing contentment and concord to flourish where conflict once persisted. A specific strategy to enhance this practice is the implementation of a weekly 'Gratitude Circle,' where each family member takes a moment to express what they are grateful for about each other. This could be done during a family dinner or a dedicated meeting. Such a ritual provides a structured opportunity for expressing appreciation and strengthens the family's emotional connections, ensuring gratitude becomes a lived value rather than a momentary gesture. Families can cultivate a culture of love and gratitude that improves relationships and well-being by embracing thankfulness in daily life.

As a result, these practices establish the foundation for encouraging support, understanding, and communication within the family. Families may face life's ups and downs together by prioritizing these factors, which will help them become more resilient and enhance their relationships. In the end, families can establish a loving and caring atmosphere where each member feels appreciated, understood, and respected by putting these tactics into practice.

Building Resilience in Family Dynamics: Prioritizing Communication, Empathy, and Adaptability

Building a good and long-lasting family environment requires a significant emphasis on empathy, communication, and adaptability. As the dynamics within a family shift over time, these fundamental principles play an essential role in ensuring that the unit remains united and supportive of each member. Effective communication is the lifeline that allows for the expression of ideas, feelings, and needs, fostering an atmosphere where each person feels valued and understood. Empathy deepens these connections, enabling family members to share in each other's joys and challenges with genuine understanding and compassion.

Moreover, when families encounter different life phases and unforeseen circumstances, the ability to adapt to novel circumstances and obstacles is essential. This adaptability helps the family deal with setbacks with fortitude, fostering their growth rather than their disintegration. Together, these elements contribute to a foundation of trust and mutual respect, which are vital for a thriving family dynamic. By committing to these values, families can create a supportive and enriching environment that celebrates individual growth while maintaining a robust collective bond.

Communication: The Foundation of Family Dynamics

At the heart of effective family communication lies the concept of active listening. This involves more than just hearing the words that are spoken. It means engaging fully with the speaker, offering nonverbal cues such as nodding and eye contact, and providing feedback that confirms the message has been received and understood. When family members actively listen to one another, they create an environment where individuals feel valued and understood, paving the way for stronger bonds and more profound connections.

Furthermore, it's critical to comprehend the distinct communication styles of each family member. This variation in communication styles can be seen in how people express their emotions when they prefer to talk about particular subjects and even when they feel most comfortable sharing their ideas and feelings. Recognizing and respecting these differences is essential for creating an inclusive family atmosphere where everyone can express themselves in a way that feels natural to them.

Setting aside specific times for family dialogues is a strategy that cannot be overstated. These designated moments, free from the distractions of daily life, allow families to come together and share their lives. Whether it's a weekly dinner where everyone discusses their week or a monthly meeting to talk about more significant issues and plans, these gatherings are vital. They ensure that all family members have a voice and that important matters are discussed collectively, reinforcing the notion that each person's input is valuable and that decisions are made as a unit.

A quote by George Bernard Shaw highlights the essence of communication within families: "The single biggest problem in communication is the illusion that it has taken place." This reminder highlights how crucial it is to make sure that family communication goes beyond surface-level exchanges and instead reaches a point where sincere comprehension and connection take place.

Families can maneuver through life's obstacles and transitions with grace and harmony if they adopt these values. Good communication becomes more than just a tool for interaction when it is based on active listening, empathy, and respect for individual differences. It becomes the cornerstone of a loving, supporting, and unified family. Families can foster a caring atmosphere that promotes the growth and well-being of all of its members and guarantees that the ties that bind them last throughout time by committing to candid, meaningful, and open communication.

Empathy: Understanding and Sharing Feelings

Empathy, the capacity to grasp and share the emotions of another, stands as a pivotal pillar in the architecture of family relationships. This profound quality fosters a strong emotional bond that unites family members and builds a foundation of support and understanding beyond just enabling sympathy. Empathy closes gaps and mends invisible wounds by turning the abstract idea of love into concrete deeds and responses.

The first step in cultivating empathy in the family context is for parents and guardians to lead by example. More than merely actively listening, demonstrating empathy entails connecting with the speaker's feelings, validating their experiences, and answering with sincere concern and understanding. Setting an example and modeling sympathetic conduct teaches siblings and kids the importance of emotional intelligence. It's about walking a mile in someone else's shoes, not just to see the world as they do but to feel it as they feel it.

Moreover, empathy extends Its reach into resolving conflicts, standing as a catalyst for understanding and reconciliation. When disagreements arise, as they inevitably do within the closeness of family life, addressing these disputes with empathy allows all parties to see beyond their perspective. This approach fosters an atmosphere where solutions are born from a place of compassion rather than contention, smoothing over rough patches with the balm of mutual respect and understanding.

Empathy in nurturing a supportive family environment cannot be overstated. It is the glue that holds the family together, enabling members to forge connections beyond the superficialities of daily living. Through empathy, families can build a haven where every member feels seen, heard, and valued—where the emotional climate is warm and conducive to growth.

To summarize the essence of empathy in a family context, one might turn to the idiom *"to put oneself in another's shoes."* This phrase eloquently captures the core of empathetic interaction—striving to understand and feel from another's viewpoint, thereby enriching the family's emotional environment. Empathy, in its purest form, is about transcending one's ego to embrace the emotional realities of others, thereby fostering an environment where love, understanding, and mutual respect flourish.

Adaptability: Facing Changes Together

Adaptability in a family setting is like sailing a ship through constantly shifting waters. Life's journey involves several transitions, each presenting new opportunities for development and overcoming obstacles. A family's ability to collectively adjust its sails to the winds of change makes it adaptable—it keeps the ship of family unity afloat even in choppy waters.

Families need stability, but they also have to accept that change is inevitable. This contradiction necessitates a careful balance, making flexibility an essential skill. It's about more than just surviving the storm; it's about learning to dance in the rain. Whether it's the arrival of a new family member, a geographical move, or a transition in family roles, each change presents an opportunity to strengthen familial bonds through shared experiences and mutual support.

The first step in fostering an adaptable culture in a family is honest communication. Making all family members feel heard and included involves discussing impending changes and sharing their opinions and worries. This inclusive approach strengthens the notion that all family members are essential to charting their future by fostering a collaborative decision-making process.

Being adaptable also entails being accommodating to traditions and routines. Life changes may require modifying cherished family practices or inventing new ones that are more appropriate for the circumstances. This adaptability guarantees that traditions continue to be significant and inclusive, encouraging a feeling of continuity and kinship among family members.

A family's adaptability is primarily dependent on its members' creativity. Thinking with creativity might open up fresh options for action when faced with obstacles one might not have thought about. In addition to addressing current problems, this creative problem-solving promotes a proactive and inventive response to upcoming developments.

In family life, adaptability is best described by the expression "rolling with the punches." This expression captures the spirit of adaptability and resilience, highlighting the significance of changing with the times rather than fighting against it. This approach allows families to handle life's ups and downs with grace and harmony.

Building a resilient family dynamic aligns with the principles of Stephen R. Covey's key work, "The 7 Habits of Highly Effective People." Covey highlights the value of understanding before being understood, which sums up how to communicate empathetically in families. This principle emphasizes how important it is to listen to family members actively and sincerely and understand their viewpoints and feelings before offering advice and one's own opinions.

Covey's lesson highlights the importance of establishing a compassionate and unified atmosphere within families. The key to achieving this is prioritizing understanding over advice. When family members feel supported and included, they develop the interpersonal skills necessary to navigate the challenges of the outside world with dignity and grace. Covey's ideas offer a fundamental road map for families looking to improve their relationships through the power of empathy, communication, and adaptability. By adopting these principles, families can create lasting and successful connections.

Chapter 7: Identity and Self-Worth

"To dare is to lose one's footing momentarily. To not dare is to lose oneself." Soren Kierkegaard, with his deep insight into the human condition, introduces us to the essence of facing our fears head-on, particularly as we advance beyond the age of 55. This quote captures the apprehension surrounding the loss of one's sense of self and value in later years. The concern about this loss goes beyond the surface, delving into the existential dread that accompanies major life changes.

As we grow older, we frequently face challenges that question our established views of who we are and our values. Our roles and responsibilities, whether in our careers, family, or society, start to change or diminish over time. This transformation can evoke a profound sense of disorientation and loss. How does the fear of losing your anchored sense of identity shape your view of yourself? Moreover, how does it impact your sense of value in a rapidly changing world?

The crux of this fear lies in the uncertainty of redefinition. For decades, our identities may have been closely tied to external achievements and roles. As these begin to shift, the question of "Who am I without them?" surfaces with unsettling frequency. This introspective inquiry can lead to a fear of invisibility or irrelevance, as societal narratives often emphasize youth and productivity as primary sources of value.

This fear is heightened by the physical changes that come with getting older. The visible signs of aging can serve as constant reminders of the unstoppable passage of time, intensifying the worry about our position in a society that idolizes youth. This confrontation with our mortality can exacerbate the fear of losing our essence—our vitality, independence, and the unique traits that have defined our personalities over the years.

This fear intensifies with the physical transformations that aging brings. The clear signs, like wrinkles, grey hair, and the slow decline in muscle firmness, act as continual reminders that time keeps moving forward. This reality can heighten our concerns about fitting into a world that often prizes youth above all. Noticeable changes, like needing glasses to read the fine print, or the occasional forgetfulness, like misplacing keys, show the impact of each passing year. Joint stiffness in the morning or the need for more rest can subtly signal our advancing age. Facing the inevitability of our own mortality can deepen the worry about losing the energy, independence, and unique characteristics that define us.

In the words of Dylan Thomas, we see a reflection of this struggle against the fading light:

"Do not go gentle into that good night,

Old age should burn and rave at the close of day;

Rage, rage against the dying of the light."

And yet, in these changes, there's a beauty to be acknowledged, as captured by Robert Browning:

"Grow old along with me! The best is yet to be,

The last of life, for which the first was made."

These verses capture the conflict between the inherent apprehension of getting older and the opportunity for development and beauty in this inevitable aspect of life. They serve as a powerful indication that despite the visible effects of time on our bodies, our inner selves can shine with a brilliance that comes from a lifetime of experiences and knowledge.

Moreover, the loss of contemporaries, friends, and family members as we age vividly reminds us of our own vulnerability. It challenges our sense of continuity and belonging in the world, intensifying the fear of becoming disconnected from the interconnected elements that shape our lives. This experience, akin to losing pieces of a puzzle, can leave us feeling incomplete and adrift. Each goodbye adds to a growing sense of isolation, making the social scenery seem increasingly unfamiliar. Such losses not only highlight our finiteness but also compel us to confront the reality of our own aging process, prompting us to question the legacy we will leave behind.

However, it's crucial to dig into the essence of this fear. It's not merely about the loss of what was but the anxiety of facing the unknown. What will life hold when the familiar markers of identity and value are no longer as prominent? This existential uncertainty can lead to a questioning of our worth and purpose.

As we contemplate these shifts, two pivotal questions arise for self-reflection: How do you grapple with the changing dynamics of your identity as you age? And, how do you perceive your value in a society that often overlooks the contributions and wisdom of its older members?

The fear of losing one's sense of self and value in the later years is a complex concern, touching on aspects of identity, societal contribution, and existential worth. It's a reflection of the deeper struggles we face as we journey through the latter stages of our life's journey, challenging us to confront and redefine what truly constitutes our essence and worth.

The essence of identity, how we see ourselves and how we believe we are perceived by the world, undergoes a shift during this stage. The once solid ground of our self-concept begins to feel unsteady as if the very core of our being is being questioned. This period of life forces us to confront the reality that our physical selves and perhaps our cognitive abilities might not be as sharp as they once were. The reflection in the mirror portrays someone who appears recognizable yet altered, creating a feeling of disconnection from oneself.

This estrangement can prompt us to reassess our self-worth and society's perception of us. Our achievements and responsibilities that used to make us feel proud and accomplished may no longer be available in the same manner, leading us to seek new sources of self-worth and acknowledgment. The concern about losing importance, about becoming less noticeable in a culture that values youth and outward success, can be a strong motivator, leading to emotions of isolation and worthlessness.

However, the chance for profound personal development is found within this very challenge. Finding balance is key—acknowledging the losses while also celebrating the gains that come with age. There is a richness in the accumulation of years, a depth of experience and wisdom that is unique to those who have traversed many decades of life. Recognizing and valuing these qualities in oneself and in others can be a counterweight to the fears of loss and irrelevance.

The societal conversation about aging and worth is evolving gradually, yet it frequently overlooks the ongoing contributions of older individuals in various aspects such as work, volunteerism, mentorship, and sharing knowledge and life experiences. This underestimation can worsen the fear of losing one's sense of self and purpose. However, there is strength in questioning these narratives, in affirming the value of every phase of life, and in discovering new ways to make a difference and build relationships.

Many share concerns about losing our identity and worth as we grow older, but they are also very personal. It encourages us to reflect and ultimately reconsider the factors that define our identity and purpose. This redefinition can be a cause of stress but also of freedom, allowing us to explore new interests, strengthen our connections, and savor the joy of the current moment.

Strategies to Address the Fear of Aging

As we transition from understanding the fear of losing our sense of self and value in the later years, it's vital to explore strategies that can help address these concerns. Aging, a natural part of life, brings its set of challenges but also opportunities for growth and fulfillment. The key lies in adopting a proactive stance toward the changes we face, cultivating resilience, and redefining our sense of purpose and identity in positive and life-affirming ways.

Outlined below are some strategies to effectively confront and alleviate the fears linked with aging to enrich life quality and nurture a sense of contentment during later stages.

1. Adopting a Positive Outlook

Cultivating a positive outlook entails cherishing the present moment and its pleasures, such as relishing nature walks, practicing mindfulness or meditation daily, and exploring pastimes like art or culinary endeavors. This approach not only enhances our daily experiences but also changes our outlook to appreciate the worth and charm of the aging process. Engaging in community activities, enjoying time with loved ones, or relishing peaceful moments can deepen our gratitude for life's experiences. By highlighting these uplifting moments and the insights they provide, we can cultivate a stronger and happier mindset for navigating the future, enabling us to confront transitions and obstacles with assurance and poise.

2. Staying Physically Active

Integrating consistent physical activity into our daily schedule is crucial not only for preserving our well-being but also for gaining authority over the aging process. By establishing realistic fitness objectives, we can enjoy the fulfillment of achieving them, leading to increased confidence and belief in our abilities. This empowerment is a crucial component in approaching aging with a proactive and optimistic attitude.

3. Engaging in Lifelong Learning

Committing to continual learning is an assertion that our capacity for growth and advancement never diminishes. It contests the belief that aging constrains our ability to acquire new skills or indulge in new pastimes, such as digital photography, coding, creative writing, or even mastering novel technologies like 3D printing and virtual reality. This continual involvement in learning keeps our minds sharp and our spirits buoyant, nurturing a youthful inquisitiveness that enriches our later stages of life. Whether it's taking online courses in environmental science, joining a pottery class, or participating in a local history group, these learning experiences expand our horizons, keep us connected with current trends, and significantly contribute to a fulfilling and vibrant life.

4. Fostering Social Connections

Actively nurturing social connections involves pushing ourselves to interact with new individuals or strengthening existing relationships. For example, joining a local club or community group can introduce us to new friends who share our interests and values. It's about establishing a support system that offers mutual care and understanding. These connections serve as our foundation, providing the necessary emotional backing and camaraderie needed to traverse the impediments of getting older.

5. Embracing Volunteerism

Volunteering provides a distinct blend of social engagement, skill application, and the profound gratification of contributing to the greater good. Activities such as guiding young learners, participating in community cleanup endeavors, conducting workshops at local libraries, or aiding in animal shelters not only enable the utilization of lifelong skills but also encourage the acquisition of new ones. Engaging in diverse volunteer undertakings helps bolster our role as valuable members of society who can effect meaningful changes. Having a clear sense of purpose can significantly alleviate the apprehension of feeling irrelevant or inconsequential as we age by showing the various avenues through which we can still have a positive impact on our communities.

6. Practicing Mindfulness and Reflection

Practicing mindfulness and reflection aids in embracing the transformations that accompany aging rather than opposing them. It teaches us to appreciate the present moment, approaching each experience with an open and curious mind. This acceptance can result in a deep sense of peace and contentment, countering the anxieties that frequently come with getting older.

7. Seeking Professional Support

Turning to experts shows our commitment to living our best lives, no matter our age. Sharing a problem can reduce its weight, emphasizing the significance of seeking assistance when necessary. It's a recognition that as we get older, we face certain difficulties, but there are tools out there to support us along the way. Professional guidance can equip us with the tools needed to rebuild our sense of self and address the emotional complexities of aging, reminding us that seeking support is not a sign of weakness but a step toward empowerment and resilience.

8. Redefining Purpose

Exploring new horizons and redefining our purpose in later life can lead us to delve into areas of interest or passion that we may not have had the opportunity to explore before. This encourages us to delve into areas of interest or passion that may have been overlooked due to a lack of time or courage in our years. It prompts us to reconsider what holds significance and how we choose to invest our time, efforts, and skills. Exploring pursuits like learning to play instruments, participating in book clubs, exploring genres, or even launching a small business centered around a lifelong passion can brighten this path. Moreover, engaging in advocacy for issues that are important to us, such as improving education, promoting animal welfare, or fostering community development, can bring a sense of achievement and connection. This exploration, driven by the desire to contribute and evolve, can lead to a revitalized sense of purpose and contentment, demonstrating that aging can be a phase of growth and revelation.

Addressing the fear of aging is a multi-dimensional endeavor that requires a holistic approach, encompassing physical health, mental well-being, social connectivity, and emotional resilience. *"Age is an issue of mind over matter. If you don't mind, it doesn't matter,"* Mark Twain once quipped, highlighting the power of attitude in shaping our experience of aging. By adopting a comprehensive approach to navigating the transitions that accompany aging, we can shift the experience from one tinged with apprehension to one filled with anticipation and joy, demonstrating that the later years hold potential for fulfillment. This transformation not only enriches our well-being but also serves as an inspiring model for others, showcasing that aging can be embraced with elegance and energy.

Embracing Growth Beyond the Golden Years

In the heart of a bustling city lived Charles, a seasoned executive who had spent decades in the corporate world and was now considering the next chapter of his life post-retirement. Across town, there was Evelyn, a retired school teacher who had always poured her heart into her students and her community. Both were at a point where societal expectations of "slowing down" didn't match their desires for personal growth and fulfillment.

Charles, after reading "Tuesdays with Morrie," started to reflect on the purpose of his years of dedication and whether he was truly able to savor the rewards of his efforts. He yearned to rediscover his initial enthusiasm for the environment, a passion that his career goals had eclipsed. His newfound passion for environmental causes inspired him to use his leadership skills to champion conservation efforts and make a difference in the battle against climate change.

Evelyn, on the other hand, found herself at a crossroads after retirement. With additional time available, she returned to her fondness for painting, an interest she had put aside for her profession and family. Taking motivation from her days as an educator, she commenced providing art workshops to youngsters in her locality, combining her enthusiasm for teaching with her affection for art. This initiative not only satisfied her desire for artistic expression but also maintained her involvement in the pleasure of teaching.

Charles and Evelyn's adventures, each following a unique path, underscore the common theme of welcoming personal development at any point in life. Charles's move from a corporate executive to an environmental advocate demonstrates the possibility of exploring new ways to make a difference outside of work. At the same time, Evelyn's change to teaching art showcases the happiness of reconnecting with and spreading forgotten interests.

Their stories push back against the idea that personal development is only for the young, emphasizing that it's always possible to follow your passions and have an impact. They ask important questions to individuals facing a decision: What interests have you set aside while focusing on your professional life? How can you utilize your skills and experiences in fresh, rewarding ways?

Through Charles and Evelyn, we are reminded of the significance of self-reflection and taking steps to create a life that aligns with our authentic selves. The stories inspire us to probe into our interests and make a difference in our communities, demonstrating that self-improvement and satisfaction can thrive, particularly in the later stages of life.

Charles and Evelyn's stories emphasize the importance of continuing personal growth at any stage of life, especially after reaching the age of 55, when societal norms may suggest slowing down. Their stories are a powerful reminder that personal development is an ongoing process, replete with chances for growth, discovery, and creating a significant influence.

Embracing personal development involves acknowledging that each phase of life presents distinct chances to discover interests, connect with different groups, and make meaningful contributions aligned with our core beliefs. It's about seizing the opportunity to rediscover aspects of ourselves that we may have overlooked and discovering delight in new pursuits.

Reflecting on their stories encourages us to contemplate our journeys. What are the passions waiting to be discovered? How can we leverage our skills and experiences to create an impact? By asking these questions, we unlock a world of possibilities, demonstrating that the journey toward personal development has no age boundaries.

By embracing personal growth, we can enrich our lives and inspire others to see every moment as a chance for discovery and transformation. As Maya Angelou beautifully expressed, *"You can't use up creativity. The more you use, the more you have."* Let the stories of Charles and Evelyn motivate you to start your personal growth journey, fully enjoy every stage of life, and welcome the countless opportunities that await.

Chapter 8: Mortality and Existential Dread

Contemplating the end of one's life raises a question: Have you ever thought about how your mortality impacts your life? This reflective process, though seemingly serious, serves as a catalyst for gaining an understanding and appreciation for our existence. Recognizing the nature of our time motivates us to live purposefully, encouraging us to embrace each moment with enthusiasm and direction.

The journey toward accepting our finite existence reshapes our worldview, influencing our decisions and priorities. It encourages a thoughtful exploration of what truly matters in our lives. Chasing after material possessions and achievements cannot match the value of building strong relationships, seeking personal satisfaction, and creating a lasting legacy. This new outlook encourages us to live with purpose, making choices that align with our values to cultivate happiness and satisfaction.

This heightened consciousness brings the present moment into sharper focus. In today's fast-paced world, where we often find ourselves lost in reflections of what was or anxious about what might be, acknowledging the brevity of life anchors us in the immediacy of now. This realization fosters gratitude, urging us to cherish life's simple joys—a meaningful conversation, the serenity found in nature, or the happiness that comes from pursuing our passions. Such moments, when fully appreciated, significantly enrich our existence.

"Death is not the opposite of life, but a part of it."

-Haruki Murakami

Take the global reflection prompted by the pandemic; this period, characterized by widespread loss and uncertainty, vividly highlighted the fragility of life, echoing Murakami's observation that life and death are inseparable aspects of human existence. The pandemic, a collective encounter with the proximity of mortality, urged many to reevaluate their lives, priorities, and the essence of living fully.

During this time, the kind of resilience stated by Murakami became more apparent and essential than ever. People and communities worldwide faced unprecedented challenges, from health alarms to financial troubles and intense feelings of being alone. Despite these struggles, the resilience of the human spirit was evident. People found new ways to stay connected, support one another, and keep going against all odds. This ability to adapt and the strength to continue is a natural part of life, often leading to personal growth, stronger bonds, and a refreshed sense of what's important.

Moreover, realizing that we all share the same fate could lead to a society built on kindness and understanding. Knowing that everyone will face the same end can break down walls like economic differences, cultural divides, or personal opinions, creating a feeling of togetherness and mutual respect. This common understanding can inspire acts of kindness and work together, helping build a more caring and supportive community.

Still, confronting our own mortality is naturally hard. As an old saying goes, *"Even the bravest man in the world fears death, but the coward dies a thousand times before his death."* It takes courage to face the fears and uncertainties that come with thinking about our end. But, it's through facing these thoughts that we find clearer purpose and direction. It compels us to ponder deeply on our values, the legacy we aim to leave, and the impact we wish to have on the world and the lives of others.

The observation of our mortality is not merely an exercise in acknowledging the inevitable but an opportunity to live with heightened awareness and authenticity. It urges us to make our lives of significance, ensuring every choice, relationship, and moment is filled with purpose and meaning. While the thought of our demise might scare us, it also stands as a strong motivation to appreciate our time, live generously and kindly, and create a legacy that mirrors our truest beliefs and desires.

Approaching Mortality and Existential Dread in Later Life

"The greatest discovery of any generation is that a human being can alter his life by altering his attitude."

*- **William James***

In the journey beyond 55, individuals are presented with a unique opportunity to redefine their relationship with the world around them. This stage of life, often accompanied by reflections on personal legacy and the nature of existence, calls for a thoughtful reassessment of what it means to live fully in the face of our finite time.

Here, we explore various strategies to confront and engage with these existential realities in a constructive and meaningful way.

1. Embracing Mindfulness and Present Living

Living in the moment and practicing mindfulness can be a potent antidote for dealing with worries about dying. This approach encourages a full and present-oriented living, where the fleeting essence of life is not only recognized but also joyfully experienced. One's present-moment experiences can be further enhanced by practices that support this mentality, such as focused music listening or partaking in sensory exercises like slowly and deliberately tasting food. Engaging in these activities helps people to stay present in the moment while also creating a place for happiness and contentment that goes beyond material worries.

2. Legacy and Meaning Creation

Leaving a legacy and seeking purpose can take many different shapes, each reflecting the individual's values and goals. Beyond giving back to the community and serving as a mentor, other individualized ways to transmit wisdom and love include writing letters to the next generation or capturing personal tales in video diaries. By acting as a bridge to the future, these sharing gestures enable people's wisdom and experiences to live on and influence others long after their own lives have ended. They represent the aspiration to make a meaningful and long-lasting difference in a world that endures beyond our bodies.

3. Building and Strengthening Relationships

At the heart of our existence are the relationships we nurture, which assume heightened significance as we confront the reality of our mortality. Initiating community-oriented projects or embarking on journeys with loved ones not only fortifies these connections but also creates a repository of collective memories. These endeavors show the value of solidarity in the face of life's fleeting nature, forming a legacy of communal affection and shared humanity that triumphs over time.

4. Acceptance and Emotional Resilience

Cultivating acceptance of life's finality and resilience necessitates a journey into vulnerability, discovering potency within its embrace. Engaging in communal support structures or going into creative arts therapies provides channels for articulating and wrestling with the complex web of emotions tied to existential ponderings. Through these collective and creative expressions, individuals find solace and strength in the camaraderie of shared experiences, fostering a sanctuary of mutual understanding.

5. Continuous Learning and Growth

A steadfast commitment to perpetual learning and self-betterment echoes the sentiment that the pursuit of personal growth does not wane in the shadow of mortality but gains even greater urgency. Immersing oneself in online learning communities or collaborative creative ventures not only widens one's intellectual and experiential horizons but also cultivates enriching connections. This path of relentless curiosity and self-refinement underlines the conviction that growth is an infinite quest, imbuing every phase of life with purpose and fulfillment.

6. Health and Wellness

The pursuit of health and vitality within the framework of life's finiteness embraces a comprehensive strategy toward achieving wellness. Incorporating practices such as conscious nutrition and joining in collective fitness activities not only improves physical fitness but also cultivates community cohesion and a united goal. These practices emphasize the belief that maintaining one's physical and psychological health is a crucial gesture of self-esteem and a recognition of the significance of existence.

7. Philosophical and Spiritual Exploration

Understanding philosophical and spiritual dimensions offers profound insights into the essence of being and our place within it. Engaging in dialogues across different faiths or participating in philosophical circles can broaden one's view, offering diversity. These investigations promote a deeper comprehension of mortality—not as a means of demise but as a basic feature of the human condition that calls us to live intentionally, sensibly, and compassionately.

In addition to providing a way through existential realities, each of the above strategies emphasizes that transformation and fulfillment are possible at any point in life. This highlights the age-old truth that our attitude affects our path and that every moment is an opportunity for growth and regeneration. Life after 55, therefore, ceases to be seen as a time of decline and instead presents itself as a time for enrichment, discovery, and profound interaction with the world.

The Transformative Power of Mortality Awareness

Understanding the transient nature of our being initiates a deep reflection on the manner in which we engage with our surroundings and the broader community. Such an insight often catalyzes a profound empathy and interconnectedness, propelling us toward actions that are inherently kind and understanding. As we delve into this topic, it becomes apparent that recognizing the short span of our lives profoundly shapes our behavior in uplifting ways, nudging us toward substantial contributions. This realization breeds a culture where compassion is the bedrock of social interactions, paving the way for a world that's more empathetic and interconnected. It prompts us to transcend our variances, acknowledging the essential commonalities and collective fate that unite us, hence fostering a spirit of togetherness and common purpose.

Let's consider the example of a community initiative inspired by the recognition of life's fleeting moments:

In a small town, realizing life's short span motivated residents to initiate a community garden project. This endeavor was aimed not just at plant cultivation but at fostering unity and support within the community. The project brought together individuals of various ages and backgrounds, facilitating knowledge transfer and resources. It became a space where everyone could contribute, learn, and grow together, significantly enhancing communal bonds. Through their collective effort, they created not only a thriving garden but also a stronger, more supportive community environment, showcasing the power of collective action in creating lasting, positive impacts.

This acute consciousness motivates us to confront health inequalities and champion efforts that bolster well-being across the globe. Such a shared realization nurtures a more encompassing approach to healthcare, ensuring societies are adequately equipped to manage health emergencies and individuals receive fair medical treatment. This adjustment not only advances public health but also cements community ties as people unite in support of one another. Mobilizing toward a unified objective of health fairness lays the groundwork for a more wholesome future for everyone. This intensified focus on communal health introduces pioneering solutions that tackle the fundamental causes of health disparities, advocating a comprehensive view of health that includes physical, mental, and societal well-being.

Moreover, this comprehension heightens our preparedness and resilience against emergencies and catastrophes. In response to the devastation wrought by Hurricane Katrina in 2005, communities heavily impacted by the storm rallied together to enhance their preparedness and resilience against future emergencies. The event brought to light the critical need for more effective disaster response and recovery strategies, particularly in protecting the most vulnerable groups. In the recovery process, there was a significant emphasis on rebuilding with a focus on durability and emergency readiness.

This was achieved through collaborative efforts among municipal authorities, nonprofit entities, and the community at large, leading to the formulation of superior emergency response strategies, fortification of critical infrastructure, and optimized distribution of resources to those in dire need. These joint endeavors highlighted a shared dedication to not just reconstruct but also to cultivate a deeper sense of unity and resilience within communities, making safety and security accessible to all, especially the most vulnerable.

Recognizing our shared vulnerabilities sharpens our focus on seeking peaceful and reconciliatory solutions when addressing conflict resolution. This standpoint promotes conversation and empathy, striving to settle disagreements in ways that honor human life and nurture enduring peace. Adopting this methodology not only eases current conflicts but also aids in crafting a more stable and harmonious international community. This push for peace and comprehension highlights the value of each moment and the significance of utilizing our limited time to cultivate harmony rather than strife. It prompts a reassessment of what's truly important, prioritizing relationships and human connections over triumphs in disputes, thus building a legacy of peace for generations to come. As the proverb goes, *"A soft answer turns away wrath, but a harsh word stirs up anger,"* emphasizing the power of gentle communication in resolving conflicts and fostering lasting peace.

The role of education and the quest for knowledge gain prominence when we ponder our fleeting existence. An increasing awareness of the importance of offering universal opportunities for learning and growth is becoming more apparent. By eliminating barriers to education and promoting a culture of lifelong learning, we empower individuals to achieve their utmost potential and lead fulfilling lives. This dedication to education showcases the belief in the transformative effect of knowledge and its capacity to positively influence society. It recognizes that education extends beyond personal achievement to become a crucial instrument for societal advancement, fostering a well-informed, engaged, and competent populace.

Reflecting on these perspectives, it's clear that considering our finite time on earth encourages a shift toward more compassionate, resilient, and inclusive communities. It drives us to act intentionally, cherish our connections, and aim to shape a reality that reflects our loftiest principles. Seeing our life through this lens alters the perception of our finite days from a cause for fear to a powerful catalyst for communal advancement and beneficial change, inspiring us to establish a heritage that surpasses our lifespan. This awareness is a motivational force for change, prompting us to consider the impact we desire to create and undertake clear actions toward developing a more fair, understanding, and lasting society.

This harmonizes with the lessons from Viktor E. Frankl's "Man's Search for Meaning," in which Frankl, a survivor of the Holocaust, goes into the significance of discovering a goal in the harshest of situations and the strength of the human will to surpass adversity and discover significance in existence. His narrations and psychological observations demonstrate that confronting the truth of our finite existence encourages us to pursue a richer comprehension of our goals and to adopt lifestyles that enhance the common welfare, thereby affecting the world in significant and enduring manners. Frankl's insights underline the notion that realizing the shortness of life should inspire us to embrace lives marked by determination, goal, and dedication to the welfare of others.

Chapter 9: Personal Stories

In later years, individuals discover themselves at a crucial intersection, where the wealth of past experiences offers a distinct perspective on both their history and the future ahead. It's a period when pondering over past experiences, lessons acquired, and the insight gained becomes inherently intertwined with the expectation of future possibilities.

The process of attaining this age often comes with a deep gratitude for the journey so far. It's a moment to acknowledge the myriad experiences that have molded one's identity and perspective. This acknowledgment isn't solely about recognizing achievements or dwelling on setbacks. Instead, it's about comprehending the significance of every moment that has contributed to one's current state. This deeper acknowledgment fosters an appreciation for the life lived and the individuals who have accompanied it on that journey.

Moreover, at 55, there is a subtle realization of life's transient nature, which emphasizes the importance of living authentically and pursuing what genuinely matters. This age often triggers individuals to reassess their priorities, making decisions that mirror their true aspirations rather than societal norms or external pressures. It's a phase where the pursuit of personal satisfaction takes precedence, guided by the wisdom gained from experience.

Additionally, this significant age provides the chance to pass on knowledge and insights to younger generations. The abundance of experiences amassed by this point becomes a valuable asset, not only for personal contemplation but also for imparting to others. This act of imparting is not only about teaching lessons but also about establishing meaningful connections with others, contributing to a legacy that surpasses individual accomplishments. As the saying goes, *"By the time you're 55, you've learned a thing or two. Sharing that knowledge doesn't just lighten your load; it brightens the path for those following in your footsteps."*

There is a significant shift in the way we anticipate future opportunities. Armed with a treasure trove of experiences, individuals stand at this milestone with a perspective that is both grounded and optimistically forward-looking. This well-rounded perspective involves not only recognizing life's uncertainty but also wholeheartedly accepting it with a sense of assurance. It's a confidence that stems from overcoming numerous challenges, following passions, and valuing the relationships built over time. This knowledge imparts a strength that equips individuals to navigate upcoming journeys gracefully, no matter the challenges they may bring.

Life Lessons Learned by 55

Transitioning smoothly from this perspective to the fundamental life lessons of this important stage, it's clear how these experiences influence one's attitude toward life, relationships, obstacles, and personal satisfaction. As people embrace the chance to share their accumulated knowledge, they not only ease their own burden but also light the way for future generations. Passing on knowledge showcases the interconnectedness of generations and the lasting legacy each person can create.

The Value of Relationships

At 55, many people come to appreciate the immense importance of relationships. This stage of life reflects a growing value for relationships with family, friends, and the broader community. The connection with a lifelong friend especially stands out, representing a special mix of support, love, and shared experiences. This kind of friendship, nurtured over many years, demonstrates loyalty and mutual understanding, providing a safe haven during life's challenges. Such relationships are essential for one's overall happiness and well-being, proving the saying, *"Old friends are gold."*

Alongside the cherished connection with a lifelong friend, the relationships with one's spouse and children gain added layers of importance. The relationship with a partner transforms into an extraordinary adventure of shared moments, mutual assistance, and empathy that has endured the trials of time. This lasting bond provides a strong base of stability and affection that is priceless, capturing the essence of the quote, *"Love becomes more intense, quick, and touching as the years go by."*

Learning to forgive, especially within the context of these long-standing friendships, gains prominence with age. As we grow older, the importance of learning to forgive, especially within long-standing friendships, becomes more evident. Forgiveness is seen as a valuable gesture toward achieving personal peace and freedom, benefiting both parties involved. It entails releasing previous grievances to create space for more fulfilling experiences and emotions. This lesson in forgiveness, particularly applied to the misunderstandings and conflicts that inevitably arise in long-term friendships, can profoundly transform these relationships, making them even more rewarding and resilient.

Resilience Through Challenges

Another important lesson learned by this age is resilience—the ability to endure and recover from life's unavoidable challenges. Among various personal and professional challenges, overcoming a health scare becomes a pivotal narrative for many. Such a challenge is not viewed simply as a hindrance but as a vital factor that molds character and alters one's outlook for the positive. The journey through diagnosis, treatment, and recovery is a powerful reminder of the strength and perseverance that reside within us, carrying the essence of resilience.

These experiences, particularly overcoming a severe health challenge, often come with invaluable teachings. They underscore the significance of health, the fragility of life, and the resilience that can be discovered in our frailty. The capacity to recover from a health crisis with a revitalized sense of direction and gratitude for life emphasizes the vitality of resilience. It reminds us that, while we may not control every aspect of our lives, we have the ability to shape our responses and adaptations, discovering strength and growth amidst adversity.

Viktor E. Frankl's influential work, "Man's Search for Meaning," adds a profound dimension to understanding resilience amid challenges. Frankl's encounters as a Holocaust survivor and his observations on human behavior under extreme circumstances provide profound insights into the essence of resilience. His central idea—that the primary human impulse is not pleasure but the pursuit of what we find meaningful—is particularly pertinent here.

Frankl noted that individuals who made it through the atrocities of concentration camps often did not rely on physical strength or external factors but on their capacity to discover purpose in their pain. This perspective changes how we see resilience: it's more than just recovering from challenges, but also about discovering significance and value in the difficulties. Frankl's concept that *"When we can't alter a situation, we must adapt ourselves"* goes deeply with the essence of resilience. It highlights how our response to challenges and our capacity to derive significance from them can greatly impact our overall health and development.

The Pursuit of Passion

Reaching middle age, especially by the age of 55, frequently signifies a pivotal moment in how individuals perceive their lives and priorities. This phase engenders a deep-seated recognition of the importance of pursuing one's personal interests, a lesson that gains further clarity with the passage of time. Numerous individuals discover that this phase presents not only a chance for self-reflection but also a chance to take action—investigating unexplored passions or rekindling old ones that were perhaps disregarded amid the frenzy of earlier years.

At this point in time, the quest for passion surpasses the typical attainment of outward success; rather, it transforms into an expedition toward the discovery of intrinsic happiness and satisfaction. This concept pertains to relinquishing the constraints imposed by societal norms that frequently prescribe age-related capabilities in order to pursue those that genuinely elicit joy and fulfillment. Consider 55-year-old Thomas, who has always been passionate about music but has never taken it seriously.

Following this significant milestone, he resolved to start piano classes, an undertaking he had long desired but never pursued. The attempt to chase one's passion, which could entail mastering a different language, setting off on a solitary journey to an ideal spot, grasping a musical device, or initiating a weblog, is a crucial lifeline that revitalizes one's life with vigor, excitement, and an inherent sense of direction. The voyage of exploration and self-awareness is not exclusively motivated by personal contentment.

The journey of investigation and self-realization is not simply motivated by one's own fulfillment. Furthermore, it becomes a source of inspiration for others, showcasing that midlife can be a dynamic and fruitful period filled with potential. Participating in personal interests not only enhances one's existence but also imparts a renewed sense of vitality and drive that surpasses the traditional limitations of age, thus establishing that the quest for what elicits joy is an indispensable component of a rewarding life.

Health as a Priority

Upon reaching the age of 55, the paramount significance of health—which includes mental, physical, and emotional wellness—becomes conspicuously apparent. This milestone frequently serves as a clarion call, compelling people to give their health the utmost importance. It is the recognition that health is not a trivial component of existence but rather the fundamental basis on which everything else is constructed. The capacity to fully appreciate the later phases of life, devote oneself to one's interests, and sustain significant relationships is profoundly undermined in the absence of optimal health.

The prevailing perspectives on health in this era adopt a comprehensive approach, acknowledging that psychological and emotional well-being are equally as important as physical health. It is crucial to recognize that incorporating a well-balanced diet, consistent physical activity, and mental and emotional health-promoting practices (e.g., yoga, meditation, or therapy) into one's health strategy are not discretionary extras but rather indispensable components. An example of this can be seen in Sarah Khan, a 55-year-old marketing director who came to recognize the significance of this comprehensive approach subsequent to years of diligent labor in pursuit of career advancement. This never-ending attention to work had negatively impacted her health. She would experience headaches, fatigue, and difficulty resting on a regular basis. Sarah recognized the necessity for a change after a particularly arduous week concluded with the cancellation of a weekend vacation with her friends on account of exhaustion.

Moreover, the significance of preventative health measures is frequently emphasized at this age. Consistent health examinations, screenings, and vaccinations are essential elements of an individual's health maintenance regimen, guaranteeing early detection and resolution of any potential complications. The guiding principle of this proactive approach to health care is that disease prevention is significantly more effective than post-treatment.

The lesson is compelling and clear: prioritizing one's health is synonymous with enhancing one's quality of life and guaranteeing a maximum experience each year. It is a commitment to venerate one's body, mind, and spirit through the provision of care, attention, and reverence. In the end, the primary objective of good health maintenance is not merely to extend one's lifespan; rather, it is to prolong one's life, allowing individuals to confront the opportunities and splendors of later stages of life with vitality, happiness and fortitude.

When we reflect on the journey to 55, the following life lessons emerge as cornerstones of a life well-lived: recognizing the importance of relationships, developing resilience, pursuing pursuits, and placing health as a top priority. They serve as a reminder that although time passes inevitably, growth, understanding, and happiness are choices we make on a daily basis. The knowledge attained by this stage of life is not merely a symbol of prestige but rather a set of practical skills that provide direction for a satisfying and purposeful existence after reaching the age of 55.

Embracing Evolution: Personal Growth, Change, and Meaning at 55

"The only journey is the journey within." - Rainer Maria Rilke.

Personal growth, the acceptance of change, and the pursuit of meaning around the age of 55 constitute a significant life journey from the standpoint of developmental psychology. This period of transition represents more than a simple chronological achievement; it denotes a profound inner development influenced by personal experiences, interpersonal connections, and the quest for satisfaction.

At the heart of personal growth lies a committed dedication to self-exploration and continual improvement. By the age of 55, individuals have recognized the importance of introspection and self-awareness in navigating life's intricacies. Personal growth goes beyond merely acquiring new abilities and knowledge; it entails refining emotional intelligence, resilience, and empathy. It involves delving into one's inner depths to uncover layers of comprehension and insight that contribute to a richer, more meaningful life.

Accepting and integrating change becomes a critical aspect of navigating the constantly evolving realms of existence. By the age of 55, individuals have presumably experienced a multitude of transitions that have put their adaptability and resilience to the test, including career changes and personal relationships. The act of embracing change necessitates a mentality characterized by adaptability and receptiveness, which enables people to relinquish sentiments tied to the past and cheerfully accept novel prospects with inquisitiveness. It involves the process of reinterpreting setbacks as chances for personal development and perceiving uncertainty as a route to novel prospects, as opposed to deriving dread or anxiety from it.

Seeking meaning by the age of 55 evolves into a profound quest for significance and purpose that transcends mere material accomplishments. It entails aligning one's actions with deeply held values and aspirations, contributing to something larger than oneself. Individuals aspire to make positive change in the world through various means, including diligent service, constructive labor, and fostering relationships. The pursuit of meaning may also involve seeking solace in nature, spirituality, or artistic manifestation, as well as establishing connections with transcendental and soul-nourishing sources of inspiration that impart a sense of direction.

Moreover, the pursuit of meaning, acceptance of change, and individual development all intersect with larger cultural and societal contexts. Individuals may pause at the age of 55 to consider their legacy and the impression they would like to impart to future generations. They may feel a sense of responsibility to contribute to the well-being of their communities and address pressing social and environmental issues. This heightened awareness of interconnectedness fosters a profound sense of belonging and collective purpose, inspiring individuals to work toward a more equitable and sustainable world where their contributions can make a lasting impact.

Take the case study of John, a 58-year-old CEO at the helm of a thriving tech company, who had always prided himself on his relentless drive and unwavering focus on results. He built his career on a foundation of ambition and decisiveness, leading his company to exponential growth. However, his relentless pursuit of success came at a cost. John's personal life remained neglected, and his relationships were strained by his long hours and work-centric mindset.

After experiencing a family intervention and coming close to burnout, John had a wake-up call. He started to ponder the real significance of success and the impact it had on his health and relationships.

John set out on a quest to find himself, striving for a life that was more balanced and satisfying. He engaged in therapy to address his work-life imbalance and cultivate emotional intelligence. He also signed up for leadership development programs with a focus on nurturing empathy and enhancing team dynamics. His exploration provided him with fresh insights and resources to navigate the challenges of work and personal relationships.

Initially hesitant about embracing change, John eventually recognized its importance. He introduced flexible work arrangements for himself and his employees, encouraging a better work-life balance. He also assigned tasks more effectively, empowering his team and fostering a sense of shared ownership within the company. Although it was difficult at first, these adjustments resulted in a workforce that was more involved, higher productivity, and a more encouraging work atmosphere.

Beyond his company, John began to search for ways to make a difference in something bigger than himself. He became a member of the board of a local non-profit organization that specializes in offering educational opportunities for underprivileged youth. Guiding young individuals and observing their development brought him a deep sense of meaning and satisfaction.

John's journey exemplifies how personal development, adapting to new circumstances, and searching for purpose can intersect in the later years of life. His story emphasizes the significance of knowing oneself, being flexible, and striving for a meaningful goal that goes beyond just wealth. John's leadership approach evolved from focusing only on achieving results to emphasizing both the success of the business and the welfare of his employees. His participation in the non-profit organization enabled him to make a difference in a social cause and also helped him feel connected.

Chapter 10: Finding Purpose

Redefining purpose and meaning in later years has been a pursuit across generations, transcending professions and cultures. The journey of Benjamin Franklin, a polymath and one of the Founding Fathers of the United States, lights this path vividly. Despite the accomplishments of his early and middle years, Franklin's later life was characterized by an unwavering dedication to public service and diplomacy. Throughout his seventies and eighties, he made a significant impact on the development of the United States through his diplomatic prowess as ambassador to France, which proved indispensable in obtaining French assistance throughout the American Revolution. Franklin's life serves as an illustration of how the later years can manifest as a turning point, characterized by a transition toward pursuits that surpass individual accomplishments and make more extensive contributions to society.

In a similar way, Michelangelo's artistic trajectory, which was renowned for his ceiling paintings and sculptures for the Sistine Chapel, remained vibrant throughout his later years. His creative zeal and pursuit of new endeavors persisted instead. In his later years, he embarked on the design of St. Peter's Basilica in Vatican City, a monumental task that showcased his architectural genius. Michelangelo's engagement with this project well into his old age highlights his capacity for continuous growth and creativity, challenging the notion that the later years are a time for withdrawal.

Harriet Tubman, who led enslaved people to liberation via the Underground Railroad, is another figure of inspiration. In addition to her early involvement in direct action, Tubman devoted her later years to advocating for women's suffrage. She collaborated with notable individuals such as Susan B. Anthony and Emily Howland, advocating for women's suffrage through her words and experiences. This shift from abolitionist endeavors to women's rights activism stands as a demonstration of the capacity to redefine one's mission and make contributions to various aspects of societal transformation throughout one's lifetime.

The mentioned historical instances show the varied approaches through which individuals have reevaluated their sense of purpose and significance as they aged. Driven by a lifetime of experience and sagacity, the later years of life present a unique opportunity to pursue new objectives, be it through activism, creative expression, or diplomacy.

Individuals who prioritize introspective fulfillment over outward accomplishments are inclined to investigate and adopt novel facets of their personalities and passions. This exploration can see individuals picking up forgotten musical instruments, learning new languages, or diving into digital technologies, not for accolades but for the sheer joy of learning and personal expansion. Such endeavors are not just hobbies but pathways to reinvigorating a sense of identity and capability, often leading to unexpected avenues of creativity and innovation.

In this stage of life, the idea of contributing positively gains renewed importance, evolving from a duty into a source of happiness and meaning. Participating in community activities or guiding younger individuals becomes a means to distribute knowledge and past lessons, building a legacy of impact and motivation that surpasses work-related successes. Such involvement frequently leads to a feeling of inclusion and making a difference, enhancing the person's connection to the broader communal story. This shift highlights the fulfilling nature of altruism, emphasizing how personal fulfillment can be intertwined with the well-being of others.

The reflection on legacy shifts toward a focus on the enduring impact of one's values and actions beyond material wealth. This could manifest in the cultivation of a family garden that becomes a symbol of growth and sustainability for future generations or the establishment of a local book club that fosters a love for reading and community connection. Such acts, though seemingly small, carry profound implications for how individuals wish to be remembered and the values they hope to perpetuate.

Acknowledging the limits of life encourages a more discerning use of time, emphasizing profound, significant interactions rather than shallow activities. This could involve giving importance to family reunions to strengthen connections with loved ones or beginning spiritual pilgrimages to Santiago de Compostela or Mecca, which can provide a feeling of peace and satisfaction. Engaging in such activities can enrich the soul and reinforce connections with one's heritage and beliefs.

Discovering new purpose and significance beyond the age of 55 involves a quest for authenticity, the fulfillment of making a difference, and reflecting on one's legacy. It's a dynamic process that fosters ongoing development, introspection, and involvement, providing a diverse range of experiences that strengthen the individual's life and the lives of those around them. This stage accentuates the beauty of aging as an opportunity for renewal, discovery, and profound impact.

Approaching Your Transformative Journey

Approaching this transformative journey demands a multifaceted strategy that probes into unique and enriching experiences.

Here's a guide on traversing this significant phase of life with insights for each aspect:

1. Embrace Mindfulness and Present Living

In addition to meditation, deep breathing, and yoga, try to include mindfulness in your daily activities, like being present while eating and walking. These practices promote a greater understanding of the present, decrease anxiety, and enhance mental well-being. Documenting your experiences can also increase awareness and gratitude, enriching your path toward mindfulness. Consider maintaining a gratitude journal, jotting down three things you appreciate each day to foster a more positive perspective.

2. Foster Inter-generational Connections

Consider participating in community programs that encourage inter-generational activities to share insights and learn from younger generations. Get involved in organizing activities that unite people of various generations, like technology classes for older adults or storytelling events focused on sharing wisdom and personal stories. Organize a club where members of different generations discuss the same book, fostering shared experiences and understanding. These activities help connect people of different ages and promote respect and understanding between them.

3. Explore Volunteerism in New Domains

Aside from contributing to causes, think about using your professional skills to help nonprofits that could use your expertise on a voluntary basis. This could involve providing free consulting services or mentoring startups or young professionals. Being open to new areas of volunteering additionally has the potential to expose you to broad cultures and communities, enhancing your outlook and personal growth. Volunteer as a mentor at a local school, sharing your knowledge and inspiring the next generation.

4. Prioritize Physical Well-being

Incorporate activities like walking groups, swimming, or gentle fitness classes into your schedule for physical and social advantages. Find out nourishment workshops or culinary classes that stress healthy eating to improve your diet. Don't forget that it's essential to prioritize your mental health by participating in activities that make you happy and help you unwind, as they are vital for your overall health. Think about exploring a dance class or trying out a new sport that interests you, adding an enjoyable aspect to your physical activity.

5. Reevaluate Your Living Environment

Consider the accessibility of your home and its adaptability to changing mobility needs. Engaging in community gardening or local beautification projects can enhance your connection to your environment and foster a sense of belonging. Exploring eco-friendly living options can also align with a lifestyle that's both healthful and meaningful. Downsize to a smaller, more manageable home if needed, or consider making modifications to your current home to improve accessibility.

6. Engage with Technology

Look into apps and platforms that promote healthy living, mental sharpness, and social connectivity. Consider using technology to share your life stories and wisdom through blogs, vlogs, or digital memoirs, connecting with a wider audience and leaving a digital legacy. Virtual reality experiences can also offer travel and learning experiences from the comfort of your home. Learn a new language through an online platform or use video conferencing to connect with loved ones who live far away. One notable tool to consider is Duolingo, an online platform for language learning. Duolingo gives you a user-friendly and interactive method for acquiring new languages, guaranteeing accessibility for users of all ages. Through interactive lessons, users can gradually enhance their vocabulary and grammar skills in an enjoyable and appealing way. This tool emphasizes how technology can be utilized to enhance mental acuity by stimulating the brain with new linguistic structures and vocabulary, improving cognitive flexibility and memory.

7. Reflect on Personal Values and Beliefs

Create a vision board or write a personal mission statement to visualize and affirm your values and aspirations. Engaging in discussions or joining interest groups around philosophy, ethics, or spirituality can offer new insights and deepen your understanding. Active participation in initiatives or causes that ring with your core beliefs allows you to live your values tangibly, bridging the gap between ideation and action. Starting a meditation practice or joining a group dedicated to meditation offers a sanctuary for introspection, fostering a connection with your innermost self, and cultivating a serene mind amidst life's tumult. These practices empower you to gracefully and intentionally through life's challenges, anchoring you in principles that foster a deep sense of purpose and well-being.

8. Plan for the Legacy You Wish to Leave

Beyond memoirs and charitable foundations, consider how everyday actions reflect the legacy you wish to leave. Small acts of kindness, eco-conscious living, and advocacy work can all contribute to a meaningful legacy. Engaging in oral history projects can also capture your experiences and insights for future generations, preserving your impact. Leave handwritten notes of appreciation for loved ones or volunteer your time at an organization that aligns with your values, making a positive difference in the present moment.

9. Seek Joy in Simplicity

Create rituals that celebrate the simple joys in life, like a tranquil morning tea in the garden or reflective evening walks.

Begin the practice of journaling to capture and ponder over the happiness found in everyday moments. As Hans Christian Andersen beautifully articulated, *'Just living is not enough... one must have sunshine, freedom, and a little flower.'* Let gratitude flow freely toward others, strengthening bonds and elevating your collective joy. Embrace mindfulness during meals, savoring each bite, akin to Thich Nhat Hanh's wisdom: 'When you eat, you are aware that you are eating.' This conscious appreciation of food nourishes your body and feeds your soul, cultivating a deep sense of presence and contentment in the now.

The Dynamic Path to Finding Purpose

The concept that our sense of purpose can evolve over time is deeply rooted in the adaptability and resilience inherent in human nature. This dynamic process highlights how our experiences, relationships, and personal growth profoundly influence our motivations and life direction. Initially, one's purpose might be closely tied to career achievements, societal roles, or familial responsibilities. However, as life unfolds through various stages, the essence of what we consider meaningful can undergo significant transformation.

Research in developmental psychology supports those different stages of life that come with unique focuses and obstacles. Erik Erikson's theory of psychosocial development outlines eight stages from infancy to late adulthood, each linked to particular psychological conflicts that aid in an individual's development. During early adulthood, the focus is often on the struggle between intimacy and isolation as individuals strive to form significant connections. Achieving success at this point fosters strong connections, while experiencing failure can lead to feelings of solitude and separation.

As people move into middle adulthood, Erikson addresses the conflict as generativity vs. stagnation, with a focus on making a difference in society and guiding future generations. This phase is focused on building a long-lasting impact, discovering fulfillment through productive and innovative projects, and fostering meaningful connections.

Later in life, Erikson's theory proposes a stage of introspection called ego integrity vs. despair, during which people reflect on their past experiences. The main idea now centers on assessing one's life and achievements, which can result in a sense of contentment and fulfillment for those who feel they have lived well or sadness for those with regrets and unrealized aspirations.

These changes, supported by psychological research, demonstrate how our priorities and obstacles shift, indicating a growing comprehension of life and the pursuit of a meaningful life. This framework provides a scientific basis for the idea that as we age, our sense of purpose and priorities naturally shift, emphasizing the importance of adapting and finding meaning in different life stages.

Experiences play a crucial role in this evolutionary process. Overcoming adversity, for instance, can radically alter our perspective, steering us toward new aspirations or altruistic paths. Positive experiences, such as impactful travel, educational achievements, or satisfying work, expand our worldview and redefine our place within it. The influence of significant relationships cannot be understated either, as they often inspire shifts in our priorities and goals, demonstrating the fluid nature of purpose shaped by the life we lead and the people we hold dear.

The journey of self-discovery and personal growth is perpetual, with each stage of life offering new insights that can refine or redefine our sense of purpose. This ongoing self-reflection, whether through mindfulness, therapy, or introspection, encourages alignment with a more authentic and fulfilling direction. Additionally, societal and cultural contexts shape our initial perceptions of purpose. Yet, exposure to diverse viewpoints and changing societal norms can challenge and broaden our understanding, allowing for a more personalized approach to finding meaning in life.

Two exemplary books that investigate the nature of purpose and its evolution over time are:

In "The Second Mountain," David Brooks delves deeper into the transformative journey individuals often embark upon after achieving traditional markers of success. He articulates a reflective shift in perspective that occurs when people realize the limitations of personal achievement for providing lasting satisfaction. Brooks suggests that true fulfillment comes from dedicating oneself to causes and relationships that transcend individual interests. He encourages readers to explore and commit to their community, relationships, and vocations in ways that nurture their souls and contribute to the greater good. This shift from self-centered to other-centered living marks the essence of climbing the second mountain, a journey characterized by the pursuit of moral joy rather than individual happiness.

"Drive: The Surprising Truth About What Motivates Us" by Daniel H. Pink challenges conventional wisdom about what motivates us at work and in life. Pink argues that the carrot-and-stick approach (extrinsic motivation) is less effective in today's world. He posits that intrinsic motivation—driven by the desire to do things because they matter, because we like them, because they're interesting, or because they are part of something important—is far more potent. Pink elaborates on how autonomy (the desire to direct our own lives), mastery (the urge to get better and better at something that matters), and purpose (the yearning to do what we do in the service of something larger than ourselves) are key factors that drive us. He suggests understanding and leveraging these elements can lead to more fulfilling and productive careers, businesses, and lives.

Both authors provide a new perspective on motivation and fulfillment, moving beyond conventional views of success to explore the deeper drivers of human behavior and satisfaction. Brooks emphasizes the importance of relationships and community in a fulfilling life, while Pink goes into the psychological needs that motivate us and bring us satisfaction. These works offer a thorough look at the elements that lead to a life filled with meaning, highlighting the significance of matching one's actions with personal values and the community at large.

In conclusion, this chapter emphasizes the enduring potential for growth and purpose that extends well into life's later years. Through the lens of notable figures and the exploration of shifting priorities, it becomes clear that the quest for meaning is not confined to youth but is a continual process of discovery and adaptation. This narrative invites us to view every phase of life as an opportunity for significant impact and personal fulfillment, underlining the beauty and possibility inherent in embracing change and pursuing a life aligned with evolving values and aspirations.

"As seasons cycle and years unfold,

Our stories of growth und purpose are told

Embrace each chapter, both new and old,

For in change, life's true beauty takes hold."

Chapter 11: Hobbies and Interests

Discovering new hobbies and interests at 55 can be an exciting and fulfilling endeavor. This phase of life often brings more free time and opportunities for personal growth. It's a prime time to explore activities you've always been curious about or to rediscover past passions that may have been sidelined. This exploration enhances your daily life and can lead to personal development and increased happiness.

"The only limit to our realization of tomorrow will be our doubts of today." - Franklin D. Roosevelt.

This quote captures the spirit of embracing new hobbies and interests, particularly at 55. Doubts and hesitations may arise, but they should not deter one from pursuing the many opportunities that await. This phase of life is ripe for exploration, offering a canvas to paint new experiences and create memories that enrich one's journey.

A Guide to Discovering New Hobbies and Enriching Your Life

Identifying potential interests is a crucial step in discovering new hobbies and enriching your life.

Below are key strategies to help you in this exploration:

Self-Reflection: Begin by reflecting on what you enjoy or have enjoyed in the past. Think about activities that have brought you joy, relaxation, or a sense of achievement. Consider your childhood hobbies, anything that sparked your curiosity, but you never had the chance to pursue, or even new areas you've become interested in more recently. Additionally, think about what excites you now, what topics you find yourself drawn to in books or movies, and any dreams you may have put on hold. This can guide you toward hobbies that align with your current interests and values. However, over-analysis may hinder action.

Research*:* Researching potential hobbies has never been easier with the vast resources available on the internet. Online platforms provide a vast amount of information and communities for a wide range of interests. This research can assist you in exploring new activities you may not have thought of previously. Seek out online tutorials and complimentary trials to get a feel for the activity without having to spend money upfront. Also, think about exploring blogs or watching videos of individuals who are involved in these interests to understand the community and the possible fulfillment it could provide.

Sampling: Trying something out is a great way to discover your true interest. Participate in workshops, classes, or introductory sessions offered in your local area or on the internet. These experiences can give you a practical understanding of the hobby without a major investment. Trying out various activities can uncover unknown talents or interests, leading to new experiences and connections. It's a stress-free way to interact with something different, giving you the freedom to explore without any preconceived notions.

Connecting with Others*:* Speaking with friends and family or participating in local clubs provides exposure to diverse activities and the social nature inherent in hobbies. Networking with individuals passionate about similar interests cultivates motivation and wisdom. Community groups and online forums foster novel kinships and support circuits, amplifying enjoyment derived from freshly adopted interests. Immersing within a fellowship of harmonious souls breeds a sentiment of belonging and spurs deeper exploration of new enthusiasms as tips are exchanged and triumphs celebrated communally.

Steps to Begin Your Journey

Below are the steps designed to guide you through the process of discovering and integrating new hobbies into your life:

1. Set Goals*:* Think about what you want to achieve through your new hobby. Whether it's learning a fresh skill, improving your physical well-being, or simply finding a creative outlet, setting clear ambitions can help direct your choice and keep you inspired. Additionally, ponder establishing both short-term and long-term goals to gauge your development. This could involve finishing a specific task, attaining a certain level of competence, or even showcasing your work or talents at a nearby event. These goals will offer direction and a sense of purpose to your efforts.

2. Start Small*:* It's easy to become overwhelmed when initiating something novel. Commence with small, manageable actions to avoid frustration. Bear in mind that the ambition is to enjoy the process, not to rush through it. Additionally, starting small enables you to gradually enhance your confidence and abilities, rendering the hobby more gratifying and less daunting. This approach can also mitigate the risk of burnout or losing interest too hastily, ensuring a more enduring and enjoyable journey.

3. Gather Resources: Once you've opted for a hobby, gather the necessary resources to get started. This might involve purchasing materials, registering for a class, or dedicating an area in your home to your new activity. Look for resources that can help you learn more productively, such as online forums, instructional books, or local clubs. Linking with others can furnish valuable insights and suggestions on the best supplies and practices, making your start smoother and more delightful.

4. Schedule Time: Regularly dedicating time to your new interest is crucial for developing it into a meaningful hobby. While consistency is key to building skills and deepening engagement, don't feel obligated to rigidly slot hobby time into every day. Try integrating it naturally into your lifestyle, whether that means weekends, evenings after work unwinding with a captivating project, or early mornings before a busy schedule when the mind is fresh.

5. Be Patient and Persistent: Learning something new can be challenging, and progress might be slow or stuck at times. When setbacks stick momentum or perfection seems distant, celebrate small victories to maintain enthusiasm. Remember that difficulties are natural and lead to insights; keep revisiting reasons for interest to stay motivated. Perseverance through tougher periods will prove valuable in the long run.

6. Adapt and Evolve: Your interests may change as deeper understanding develops, or related activities previously undiscovered could pique interest anew. Remain open to adapting and evolving your hobby over time. This flexibility allows shared growth, ensuring continuing satisfaction. Embrace exploration and self-discovery within your interest; unexpected rewards may emerge along winding paths.

Exploring hobbies and interests goes beyond passing the time; it's a chance for personal growth, learning, and finding happiness. Trying out activities can open doors to possibilities that can enrich your life in unexpected ways. Approach this opportunity with a mind and heart. Savor the journey of discovering what truly resonates with you.

The Benefits of New Hobbies and Interests

Engaging in hobbies offers a host of benefits that go beyond pastime. These pursuits can greatly improve one's quality of life, leading to a rounded and satisfying existence. Exploring hobbies brings about advantages, highlighting their positive effects on mental well-being, social connections, physical health, and continuous learning.

The life of Winston Churchill, the revered Prime Minister during World War II, shows how hobbies can profoundly impact an individual's life. Apart from his role, Churchill found solace in painting, a hobby he pursued later in life. Painting brought him comfort and mental respite from the pressures of leadership and the challenges of wartime. Painting provided solace and mental relief from the stresses of leadership and the burdens of war.

1. Enhanced Mental Health

Adopting new hobbies can powerfully influence mental health. Immersing fully in attention-grabbing activities acts like meditation, providing an escape from daily pressures and instilling a flow-like state where time vanishes. This absorption can notably reduce anxiety and depression, instilling tranquility and satisfaction. Moreover, mastering a new skill fosters self-esteem and confidence, igniting a sense of accomplishment permeating all life's domains. Leonardo da Vinci embodied the mental stimulation and contentment stemming from diverse interests beyond his artistic gifts.

2. Social Connections

Hobbies often facilitate the creation of ties, nurturing a sense of belonging and community. Engaging in group activities like joining a book club, sports team, or craft workshop can help you connect with people who have interests and values, ultimately expanding your circle. These interpersonal connections are especially vital in mitigating sentiments of seclusion or solitude, promoting societal well-being, and establishing reliable support systems. Prominent naturalist and explorer Charles Darwin frequently shared his findings and inclinations with a vast network of acquaintances and coworkers, thus exemplifying how pastimes can cultivate communal connections and encourage cooperative mindsets.

3. Physical Activity

Engaging in various hobbies supports physical exercise, which is crucial for maintaining wellness and energy. Involvement in pursuits such as trekking, biking, swaying, or practicing mindfulness activities strengthens not only a physical condition but also enhances emotional well-being by providing the release of endorphins, our innate mood enhancers. Regular participation in such active pastimes leads to a more wholesome way of living, assisting in controlling body weight, improving heart function, and raising overall stamina. The case of Teddy Roosevelt, a passionate nature enthusiast who frequently undertook trekking and equestrian activities, shows the beneficial effects of active pursuits on general health.

4. Continuous Learning

The pursuit of new interests is inherently tied to ongoing learning, keeping the brain alert and attentive. This journey of gaining new insights and abilities hones mental capabilities, supports the preservation of memory and enhancing problem-solving skills, and might even act as a safeguard against the mental decline associated with aging. The thrill of acquiring new knowledge reignites our sense of curiosity and wonder, introducing novel viewpoints and adventures into our existence. Consider Michelangelo, who continued to learn and experiment with new techniques throughout his life, demonstrating the enriching effects of lifelong learning on personal and artistic growth.

5. Personal Growth and Self-Discovery

Getting on new interests paves the way for personal growth and self-exploration, providing opportunities to discover hidden talents and enthusiasms. This voyage of discovery motivates people to leave their safety nets, embrace uncertainty, and explore, leading to a richer comprehension of their identity. Diving into diverse pursuits can unveil previously unrecognized abilities and affinities, enhancing a comprehensive and self-aware persona. Personalities like Frida Kahlo, who turned to painting as a means of self-expression and recuperation after a grave incident, exemplify how interests can fuel individual change and offer deep insights into one's emotional and psychological state.

6. Stress Relief and Relaxation

Hobbies provide a refuge for alleviating stress and finding peace, acting as a respite from our hectic lives. Immersing ourselves in activities purely for enjoyment allows us to temporarily forget daily stressors and responsibilities, giving our minds and bodies a moment to heal. Vincent van Gogh, for instance, found peace and stillness in painting, employing it as a therapeutic activity to manage his psychological challenges and distress. Engaging in painting, similar to the deliberate actions in knitting or the concentrated focus needed in crafting models, can transport individuals into a state akin to meditation. This act of concentrated creativity calms the mind, lowers stress, and promotes a peaceful state, showing how hobbies can be an effective strategy for reaching mental equilibrium and inner serenity.

7. Cultural Engagement and Creativity

Delving into hobbies also unlocks cultural involvement and creativity, providing a means to delve into and celebrate the global diversity of cultures. Engaging in the culinary arts connects us with worldwide traditions and tastes, whereas music and literature offer insights into the emotional and narrative dimensions of various communities. Georgia O'Keeffe's artistic journey enabled her to capture the grandeur and allure of the American scenery, fusing her distinct imagination with cultural influences. This imaginative journey enhances our individual experiences and deepens our knowledge and admiration for the varied and lively manifestations of human culture. Engaging in hobbies allows us to explore different avenues for expressing our thoughts and emotions, nurturing a sense of creativity that enables us to add our perspectives to worldwide art and culture.

The benefits of engaging in new hobbies and interests are far-reaching, touching upon every aspect of personal well-being. From bolstering mental health to facilitating social bonds, promoting activity, and continued learning, hobbies provide a holistic approach to enriching life. They offer tasks that stimulate in equal measure, satisfying multiple needs for challenge, enjoyment, and fulfillment—elements integral to balance and joy. In exploring new horizons, people uncover not only fresh fascinations but also the potential for personal evolution, wellness, and a deeper connection to the world around them.

Exploring a New Passion

The discovery of a new interest is akin to flipping open a book for the first time, uncertain of the escapades hidden within its text. This process, rich in discovery and fulfillment, is not merely about occupying oneself; it's an integral part of personal growth and well-being. By venturing into unfamiliar pursuits, we not only expand our perspectives but also uncover insights into our abilities, inclinations, and the unlimited possibilities for happiness and contentment in our lives.

1. Initial Curiosity

The path to uncovering a new interest initiates with curiosity, a flicker that fuels the urge to venture beyond the usual boundaries of our daily lives. This initial spark might be as transient as a passing thought about a hobby others relish or a deep-seated fascination awaiting the opportune moment for pursuit. This stage is about permitting oneself the chance to consider engaging in something new, laying the groundwork for a fruitful voyage of discovery.

2. Giving Oneself Permission

An essential milestone on this path is granting oneself the liberty to seek out new experiences, traverse beyond familiar territories, and welcome the unfamiliar. This step entails conquering internal obstacles like the fear of inadequacy or self-questioning. It's about understanding that personal expansion often stems from adventuring into unknown realms and that starting anew is perfectly acceptable. Iconic figures such as Leonardo da Vinci, celebrated for his unyielding quest for insight across various disciplines, exemplify the ethos of permitting oneself to explore boundlessly.

3. Navigating the Learning Curve

Patience is indispensable as one navigates the learning curve of a new hobby or interest. Every skill, from painting to playing an instrument, involves a process of gradual improvement and adjustment. Acknowledging that mastery takes time helps in maintaining motivation and resilience in the face of challenges. This phase is reminiscent of Thomas Edison's numerous experiments before the invention of the light bulb, a testament to the power of patience and perseverance.

4. Finding Flow and Absorption

The deep engagement in a new endeavor can usher in a state of flow, a period where time appears to halt, and one is wholly engrossed in the activity at hand. Such moments transform an ordinary hobby into a passion that enhances life. Mihaly Csikszentmihalyi, a psychologist who deeply investigated this condition, highlighted its notable advantages for emotional and mental health.

5. Overcoming Obstacles

Encountering challenges is a natural aspect of delving into new interests. Be it technical issues, allocating time for a new pursuit, or instances of discouragement, these difficulties assess our dedication and flexibility. Yet, overcoming these barriers not only reinforces our determination but also enriches our comprehension and appreciation for the endeavor. It's through tackling these challenges that the true value of the journey and its contribution to our growth is realized.

6. The Reward

Ultimately, the exploration of a new passion leads to profound personal growth and fulfillment. It uncovers new channels for expression, learning, and connectivity, fostering a more varied and enriched life experience. The adventure of identifying and cultivating a new interest affirms the human potential for adaptability, inventiveness, and the quest for joy.

The exploration of a new passion is a comprehensive journey that spans the initial spark of curiosity to the profound joy of deep involvement. It encompasses permitting oneself to explore, the importance of patience in the learning process, the rewards of overcoming challenges, and the fulfillment found in becoming absorbed in a new interest.

The Rewarding Experience of Travel and Exploration

Setting off on a journey to explore new destinations is a rewarding experience that transcends mere sightseeing; it's a profound interaction with the world that nurtures growth, understanding, and connection. Travel, fundamentally, provides a canvas on which individuals can sketch their distinct experiences, uncovering not only the variety of the planet but also revealing aspects of themselves previously unexplored. This venture into unfamiliar territories acts as a reflection, mirroring both the beauty of the world and the curiosity of the traveler.

At the core of travel lies the broadening of one's perspective. Venturing into diverse cultures and environments challenges preconceptions and opens the mind to new ways of thinking and existing. This immersion in the unfamiliar is more than just observing but actively engaging in the global narrative. Every interaction, from a simple exchange at a local market to a profound conversation with a new acquaintance, blends into the traveler's narrative, enriching their understanding of humanity and its numerous ways of life.

The significance of cultural immersion cannot be overstated, as it radically transforms one's experience from passive observership to active participation within humanity's rich global web. By engaging with a place's traditions, languages, and conventions, travelers develop profound respect and appreciation for diversity in all its forms. This plunge into cultural fabrics allows for authenticity, where travelers learn, adapt, and perhaps contribute to local environments. Such interactions bridge gaps between peoples, cultivating a sense of oneness and shared personhood.

Travel also stands as an educational tool that brings history, geography, and art alive. Walking through ruins of the past, seeing wonders of nature, and experiencing creative works in their native setting cultivate a tangible contact with the timelines of our world. These experiences cultivate the traveler's understanding and ignite a passion for continual discovery and learning. Each destination along the journey becomes an interactive classroom where lessons in the epic, ongoing story of our planet emerge.

Moreover, the act of traveling challenges individuals to leave familiar comfort, encouraging personal growth and resilience. Navigating novel environments, overcoming linguistic barriers, and handling unexpected scenarios build self-assurance and adaptability. These tests, faced and conquered, contribute to a deeper comprehension of self and capacities, qualities invaluable in all areas of life.

The impact of travel extends beyond the individual, influencing communities and ecosystems worldwide. Ethical travel practices foster sustainable tourism, confirming exploration does not come at the cost of natural or cultural heritages of destinations. By making conscious choices, travelers can bolster local economies, shield wildlife, and preserve the integrity of places they visit. This responsible approach confirms the wonders of the world remain accessible and preserved for prospective generations.

An often-overlooked facet of travel is the culinary journey it involves. Sampling the traditional foods of a region provides a direct route to comprehending its culture and history. Nourishment, in its essence, is a narrative of the population, their landscape, and their traditions. By sharing a meal, travelers and locals cultivate a bond transcending linguistic and cultural boundaries, highlighting the universal language of nourishment. This culinary exploration not only satisfies the palate but also deepens the traveler's contact with the places they visit, rendering each repast a memorable part of the journey.

The intricacy of the relationship between human societies and their environments can be seen through the geographical, climatic, and cultural adaptation of each constituent in a dish. For example, incorporating spices into Indian cuisine signifies the influence of past trade routes, whereas the understated nature of Japanese dishes demonstrates a profound regard for seasonal ingredients and natural flavors. Tourists can learn about the ecological and historical influences that mold these customs through active participation in regional cuisine.

Furthermore, engagement in food-related activities, such as attending cookery courses or embarking on market excursions, provides practical knowledge of indigenous cuisine and cultivates a more profound admiration for the artistry entailed in preparing customary fare. These experiences give travelers the opportunity to recreate and share the flavors of their journey with loved ones, thereby expanding the cultural exchange beyond the confines of the trip.

There are tremendous psychological advantages to deviating from the routine. Travel offers an essential diversion from the monotonous routine, presenting an atmosphere of liberation and revitalization. Returning to this state of mind can potentially reinvigorate creativity and elevate contentment and even productivity. Engaging in the preparations and anticipation of a journey can engender feelings of delight and anticipation, thereby promoting one's mental health and overall state of being. From this perspective, travel is a therapeutic journey that restores vitality, inspires healing, and transcends mere escape.

Making the Most Out of Your Travel Experience

Making the most out of travel involves more than visiting top spots; it's about becoming enveloped in local culture, linking with people, and embracing fresh experiences that enrich life in unforeseen ways. To genuinely benefit from what travel offers, one must delve beneath the surface, seeking narratives, flavors, and moments defining a place. This deeper engagement allows for a more authentic and fulfilling travel experience, transforming simple trips into transformative journeys.

1. Engaging with Local Culture

One of the key elements to maximizing travel is actively engaging with local culture. This means going beyond tourist attractions and hunting experiences, providing a glimpse into the everyday lives of residents calling a destination home. Attending local gatherings, festivals, and markets is a superb way to immerse in the native lifestyle and grasp the traditions and values shaping the community. This approach enriches the travel experience and fosters a greater sense of worldwide connection and empathy.

2. Learning the Language

While mastering a new language for each trip may be impossible, studying basic phrases can significantly enhance the travel experience. Communicating with locals in their tongue, even basically, can open doors to more meaningful interactions and show respect for the culture. This effort to connect, even if it involves mistakes and learning from them, can lead to unexpected friendships and insights. It is a simple yet powerful method to bridge cultural divides and deepen immersion in local living.

3. Connecting with Locals and Fellow Travelers

Connecting with people locally and traveling together greatly enriches the experience. Conversations, stories, and group activities provide different views and understanding. These interactions are invaluable travel tips, hidden gems, and growth sources. They turn visits into a rich mosaic of human bonds, enhancing travel with lasting memories and friendships.

4. Exploring Responsibly

Responsible exploration is crucial to making the most of travel experiences while ensuring destinations' beauty and integrity for future travelers. Showing locals respect, lessening environmental effects, and aiding the economy are important. Practices like following leave-no-trace principles, opting for eco-lodging, and buying handicrafts can cultivate sustainability and mutual benefit. One who travels responsibly enriches their trip and lends a hand to places and their settings.

5. Reflecting and Documenting

Taking the time to reflect on your experiences and to document them can enhance the value of your journey. Whether through journaling, photography, or simply pausing to absorb the moment, reflection allows you to process and appreciate the depth of your experiences. These documented memories are a treasure trove of insights and stories to revisit and share. It's a way to extend the journey beyond the physical travel, allowing you to revisit and relive those moments long after they've passed.

6. Staying Open and Flexible

The most memorable trips frequently arise from unexpected places and situations. Remaining open and adaptable allows for embracing spontaneity and discovering joy in unplanned aspects. Changing plans to attend a recommended local event or wandering without a destination, allowing room for serendipity, can lead to some of the most enriching travel experiences. In these unplanned instances, travel reveals its magic, offering surprises and delights that could never be scheduled.

7. Traveling Mindfully

Finally, mindful travel means fully embracing each moment and sensory experience at a destination. It's appreciating subtle beauty through active observation, listening to an unfamiliar soundscape, and feeling foreign textures. This immersed presence forges deeper connections, making travel more meaningful and rejuvenating. Journeying mindfully transforms transit from routine activity into a source of motivation, balance, and happiness.

In essence, making the most of your travel experience is a multi-layered endeavor that involves engaging deeply with the local culture, connecting with people, exploring responsibly, and remaining open to the countless opportunities that travel presents. By approaching each journey with curiosity, respect, and a willingness to learn, travelers can unlock the full potential of their adventures, turning each trip into a rich collection of experiences that contribute to personal growth and lasting memories.

This holistic approach to travel enhances the individual's experience and promotes a more connected, understanding, and sustainable world.

Chapter 12: Building Support Networks

A support network consists of various individuals, including family members, acquaintances, colleagues, and mentors, on whom an individual depends to receive guidance, comfort, and assistance when confronted with challenging circumstances or difficult decisions. These networks are crucial in both personal and professional domains as they establish a solid groundwork for perseverance, enhance self-assurance, and promote development. They act as a sounding board for ideas, share knowledge gained from personal experience, and offer practical and emotional assistance. Utilizing this framework is of the utmost importance when it comes to surmounting the milestones of life.

As individuals age, particularly those over 55, the significance of a robust support system becomes increasingly apparent. Such networks offer considerable benefits for mental and emotional health, acting as a safeguard against life's stressors. They help mitigate feelings of solitude and isolation, which are common in later years, enhance mood, foster a sense of belonging, and bolster self-esteem. Research indicates that strong social connections correlate with lower instances of depression and anxiety, emphasizing the therapeutic value of interconnectedness.

The health benefits of having an effective system of social support are linked to living longer and experiencing better health. Building relationships with others has been linked to various advantages, including lower blood pressure, reduced risk of heart issues, and a lower mortality rate. A study in the American Journal of Epidemiology emphasized the importance of strong social connections in improving physical health. It found that individuals with solid social ties had a 50% higher survival rate compared to those with weaker connections over a specific period.

Moreover, having a strong support system can promote healthier habits, which are essential for managing our bodies as we age. Encouragement from loved ones for regular screenings, exercise, and balanced eating is crucial in preventing chronic conditions common among older individuals. Support during illness or after a medical procedure can speed up recovery and improve health results, highlighting the importance of social connections in the healing journey.

Research also underlines the crucial role of social interactions in preserving cognitive function in aging adults. Engaging in lively conversations and dynamic group activities can reinvigorate the mind, potentially delaying dementia and improving cognitive skills. An exploration published by the International Neuropsychological Culture highlighted the protective effects of societal participation on cognitive deterioration, reinforcing the mental benefits of active communal inclusion. This involvement not only enriches the mental agility of persons but also contributes to their emotional wellness, building a positive comments loop that improves overall life satisfaction. Furthermore, constant social communication operates as a preventative measure against the isolation that can accelerate cognitive decline, thereby playing a fundamental part in the holistic health of the elderly.

Support systems are instrumental in guiding individual and professional progression, offering priceless mental, emotional, and health advantages, particularly critical as one becomes older. They enhance quality of life, contribute to longevity, and reinforce wellness, demonstrating the necessity of nurturing and maintaining strong communal connections throughout life's stages. The focus on continuous, quality social interaction is not merely advantageous but fundamental for a fulfilling and healthy life trajectory.

In professional contexts, support systems can be equally transformative, providing guidance, mentorship, and opportunities for advancement. These relationships foster a culture of learning and cooperation, which is crucial for career development. Professional networks can open doors to new opportunities, offer valuable advice, and provide critical feedback, underscoring the importance of cultivating relationships within one's field.

As we transition into the digital age, the scope for creating and sustaining support networks has significantly expanded, transcending traditional geographic limitations. Online platforms such as forums, social media, and virtual interest groups open up novel pathways for establishing supportive communities. These digital spaces complement existing networks, offering those who might be geographically isolated or seeking specific connections a sense of belonging and community. This digital dimension of support networks represents a modern adaptation to the age-old human need for connection, portraying how technology can bridge gaps and foster relationships across diverse landscapes.

Building a Support Network After 55: A Guided Approach

Acknowledging the multifaceted advantages of support systems in augmenting overall welfare, fostering resilience, and enhancing life, it becomes evident that for healthy aging, establishing a resilient support network after the age of 55 is not merely a source of solace; rather, it is an essential component. The subsequent approaches are intended to assist you in establishing and sustaining a robust network of support, thereby guaranteeing that you continue to feel connected, bolstered, and content throughout your later years.

Engage in Community Activities

Participating in community activities is a great way to meet new people who share your interests. Seek out organizations, clubs, or courses that are related to your interests or activities. Engaging in various activities such as book clubs, gardening groups, exercise classes, or art classes can foster an organic environment conducive to the formation of new alliances. Additionally, contemplate organizing an event or activity to increase community involvement. Such activities can stimulate one's sense of fulfillment and appeal to others who share similar passions. Being active in community service can not only increase one's visibility but also facilitate the formation of more connections.

1. Volunteer

Volunteering provides two benefits: the opportunity to meet people with similar values and to contribute to the community. Volunteers are always needed by organizations, and collaborating toward a common objective can foster strong connections. By supporting causes that hold personal significance for you, you will probably encounter individuals with whom you can share a more profound connection. Additionally, volunteering as a coordinator or project manager can help you develop leadership abilities and expand your professional connections, thereby enhancing your overall volunteer experience. This engagement has the potential to foster more profound relationships with both fellow students and the individuals you are assisting.

2. Utilize Technology

Technology can be a powerful tool for connecting with others, especially if mobility is a concern. Platforms like FaceTime, Skype, and Zoom allow for face-to-face interaction with loved ones. Social media platforms like Facebook Groups focused on specific interests or locations can help connect you with like-minded people. Online communities can also act as a source of support, where members exchange experiences, advice, and friendship. Generating material based on your passions or personal encounters can captivate others and spark discussions on the internet. Participating in online events or webinars is another great way to broaden your network and connect with like-minded individuals.

3. Reconnect with Old Friends

Reconnecting with individuals you've lost contact with can reignite old friendships. Life's changes can lead to drifting apart, but rekindling old connections can bring back nostalgia and comfort, providing joy and support. Planning a gathering or reunion can spark old connections and form new experiences. Furthermore, using social media to stay connected and exchange life updates can help maintain these rekindled relationships in the long run.

4. Join Support Groups

By attending a support group, one can connect with individuals who are enduring comparable circumstances. These gatherings, whether they are health-related, bereavement-oriented, or retirement-related, offer emotional support and guidance from individuals who can relate to your situation. Engaging in these groups actively, whether as a participant or facilitator, has the potential to foster stronger connections and instill a sense of direction. One can cultivate a robust sense of community and mutual support by exchanging personal anecdotes and attentively considering those of others.

5. Network at Religious or Spiritual Communities

Spiritual or religious communities provide many individuals with a sense of community and an established support system. Engaging in services, events, or groups affiliated with these communities may provide opportunities to meet individuals who hold similar beliefs and values. Participating in educational courses or community service initiatives can foster deeper connections and offer personally enriching experiences. In addition, mentoring and receiving mentoring from other members of the community can foster meaningful, long-lasting relationships.

6. Foster Inter-Generational Connection

Building relationships with people of various ages can significantly enhance one's support network. Younger individuals may provide assistance with technology and alternative viewpoints, while you may impart your wisdom and life experiences. These opportunities may be facilitated by programs that link seniors with younger cohorts. Engaging in mentorship programs or volunteering at schools are two ways to strengthen these intergenerational bonds. Attending seminars or classes that cater to a wide range of age groups can additionally offer opportunities to interact with a diverse array of individuals.

7. Regularly Attend Community Centers or Senior Centers

Community or senior centers often host a variety of activities specifically designed for older adults. These centers can serve as a meeting place for new acquaintances, skill acquisition, and resource discovery. Organizing a workshop or discussion on a subject you are enthusiastic about can facilitate communication with like-minded individuals. Taking part in social events or group travel planned by these organizations may also be a fun way to strengthen connections.

8. Consider Co-Housing or Shared Housing

Living arrangements like co-housing or shared housing showcase the importance of community and mutual support. These arrangements, where people reside together to encourage socializing and helping each other, are especially advantageous for individuals who live by themselves or seek a more connected community. By arranging frequent communal events, like dinners or movie nights, the connections within these communities are greatly enhanced. For example, community members could gather for a movie night showcasing a timeless film such as "The Shawshank Redemption." This not only offers entertainment but also encourages discussions and strengthens bonds among participants. Moreover, being involved in decision-making processes and joining community meetings guarantees that each resident's viewpoint is considered, promoting a genuinely collaborative and inclusive living atmosphere. This collaborative way of living not only strengthens the social connections within the community but also boosts the overall happiness of each person involved.

9. Be Open and Approachable

Lastly, embracing new experiences and keeping a welcoming, friendly attitude can draw others to you. At times, just being open to initiating a conversation or offering an invitation can result in valuable connections. Engaging in active listening and demonstrating a sincere interest in the stories of others can help them feel appreciated and more willing to share. Engaging in mutual activities can help solidify these new connections.

Building a support network after 55 is an ongoing process that requires openness, effort, and a willingness to step out of your comfort zone. By engaging in community activities, volunteering, utilizing technology, and exploring various social opportunities, you can create a supportive circle that enhances your well-being and enriches your life.

Maintaining Your Support Network

In the realm of sustaining and enriching your support network, especially as we transition through different phases of life, the emphasis shifts toward proactive engagement and deepening connections that are both meaningful and reciprocal. This journey of maintenance involves not only nurturing existing relationships but also expanding your circle in a way that adds value to everyone involved. As Helen Keller aptly put it, *'Alone we can do so little; together we can do so much.'* This sentiment has the spirit of our journey, highlighting the unparalleled strength found in the unity and mutual support of our networks.

1. Proactive Engagement and Consistent Communication

Maintaining your support system necessitates a proactive approach to communication. This extends beyond sporadic check-ins and embraces meaningful, frequent contacts that promote a sense of community and support from one another. Having regular communication events, like monthly get-togethers or weekly phone calls, can assist in creating a strong foundation that ensures no one is left behind. Intimate, one-on-one conversations mixed with group activities encourage a range of encounters that strengthen the group's relationship.

2. Deepening Connections Through Shared Experiences

Shared experiences, whether they come from conquering obstacles or collaborating on projects, are what hold your support system together. Organizing events that support the group's shared interests, such as clubs for a similar hobby or volunteer activity, can strengthen the network's sense of purpose and cohesion. Along with leaving enduring memories, these encounters help group members get a greater appreciation and understanding of one another.

3. Expanding Your Circle Intentionally

While maintaining current connections is important, expanding your network with new people can provide new ideas and perspectives. Joining new events or taking part in novel activities can offer chances to network with individuals who could brighten your social circle with their distinct perspectives and experiences. However, growing your network should be done carefully, ensuring new relationships fit in with the group's principles and enhance the group dynamic.

4. Fostering a Culture of Support and Appreciation

A culture of appreciation and support for one another characterizes a flourishing support network. Acknowledging and applauding members' accomplishments and efforts raises spirits and reaffirms the network's importance to each individual. For example, the network could plan a virtual celebration or send out a group congratulations message to honor a member who has successfully transitioned to a new professional phase. Maintaining a happy and encouraging atmosphere requires practicing behaviors like showing thanks, celebrating victories, and offering assistance when things get complicated. Small or huge, these actions represent the network's dedication to supporting each member on their path, encouraging a sense of community and group accomplishment.

5. Adapting to Changing Needs

The needs of the network's members and the ways by which support is provided and accepted will change as they grow. Maintaining the network's relevance and value for its members can be achieved by routinely evaluating the dynamics of the organization and being willing to modify your support strategies. Flexibility is essential to preserving a robust support system, whether it means reorienting activities, implementing fresh channels of contact, or providing resources for emerging challenges.

Essentially, keeping up a support system is a continuous process that calls for work, intentionality, and a readiness to change. You can make sure that your support network stays a powerful, encouraging, and enriching part of your life by cultivating regular communication, strengthening bonds through shared experiences, carefully growing your circle, creating a supportive culture, and being flexible enough to adjust to changing circumstances.

Effort and Time Investment

The foundation of any strong relationship is the investment of time and effort. In the context of a support network, this means actively reaching out, engaging in meaningful interactions, and being present for others. It's about more than just occasional check-ins; it's a consistent effort to be involved in each other's lives. This ongoing dedication helps build a robust support network characterized by trust, understanding, and mutual respect.

Practical Tips for Integrating Network-Building Activities into Your Daily Routine

Below are practical tips for integrating network-building activities into your daily routine:

1. Set aside specific times for outreach and follow-ups

Make time on your calendar to connect with your network, just as you do for personal growth or exercise. This may be a quick conversation with someone over lunch, a quick call during your morning routine, or a shared reflection after the day. To make sure no one feels overlooked, think about adding recurrent reminders to remind you to connect with various members of your network. This rigorous technique ensures that these important ties are consistently nurtured and helps you maintain a healthy and active involvement with your group.

2 Make use of technology to stay connected

In the modern digital age, resources like social media, messaging applications, and video chats can assist in bridging the gap between hectic schedules. Keeping in touch might be greatly aided by a brief update or a note of encouragement. In addition, planning online coffee dates or gaming sessions may give these exchanges a lighthearted and enjoyable touch that makes it simpler to maintain communication even when in-person meetings aren't feasible. By creatively utilizing these digital tools, it is possible to transform the obstacle of distance into a chance for more participation.

3 Incorporate networking into your everyday activities

Seek chances to establish and maintain relationships within the framework of your routine activities, such as asking a coworker to a walk-and-talk meeting or signing up for a local club or organization that shares your interests. You may also meet others who share your ideals and dedication to give back by volunteering for community service initiatives or attending charitable events. These activities enrich your life with new friendships and connections and deepen your sense of community and belonging.

The Importance of Patience and Persistence in Cultivating Meaningful Connections

Developing a supportive network is a marathon, not a sprint. As relationships progressively grow and change over time, patience is required. It's important to persevere, particularly when first attempts don't yield fruitful relationships immediately. Every conversation strengthens these connections, every experience shared, and every act of assistance. These relationships may grow into a rich, encouraging network offering priceless support through life's ups and downs with constant attention and nurture.

One can see how these ideas directly relate to growing a support network by drawing on Dale Carnegie's classic "How to Win Friends and Influence People," which emphasizes the significance of genuine interest, active listening, and the value of appreciation in creating meaningful relationships. As Carnegie advises, ties may be greatly strengthened by expressing interest in others and recognizing their accomplishments. Similar to the enduring lessons found in Carnegie's teachings, these connections may develop into a rich, supportive network that provides invaluable support through all of life's ups and downs with ongoing care and nurture.

Building and sustaining a support system takes time and commitment, but the benefits to one's emotional, social, and occasionally even physical health are substantial. People may create a strong, supporting circle by setting aside particular times for networking activities, using technology wisely, incorporating relationship-building into everyday activities, and approaching the process with patience and determination. This network is invaluable, providing support, consolation, and camaraderie, highlighting the significance of every financial commitment in these connections.

In conclusion, the essence of cultivating and maintaining a support network lies in the consistent, intentional effort we invest in fostering reciprocal, supportive, and enriching connections. Through proactive engagement, leveraging technology, and integrating relationship-building into our daily lives, we can create a resilient support system that enhances our well-being and provides a solid foundation for personal and professional growth. As we traverse life's challenges and celebrate its milestones, the strength and comfort we derive from our support network accentuate its invaluable role in our journey, making every effort toward its nurture and maintenance truly worthwhile.

Chapter 13: Physical Fitness and Well-Being

"Age is no barrier. It's a limitation you put on your mind."

-Jackie Joyner-Kersee

Maintaining physical health and well-being becomes increasingly vital as people surpass the age of 55, entering a time where prioritizing bodily prosperity is not only advantageous but crucial. The gradual process of aging affects numerous body functions, necessitating the choice of a lifestyle enriched with regular exercise. Such practices can significantly shape overall wellness, leading to improved mobility, a decreased chance of persistent illnesses, and better mental health, thus securing an enriched quality of life in these stages.

With the progression into later years, our bodies inevitably undergo transformations, such as diminishing muscle mass, lowered bone strength, and an elevated risk of persistent conditions like cardiovascular disease, diabetes mellitus, and joint inflammation. These shifts can profoundly influence physical capabilities and overall health. Yet, regular participation in exercise can mitigate these effects. Integrating physical activity into everyday life, the elderly can preserve muscular strength, control their weight more efficiently, and lessen the risk of various health problems related to aging, establishing exercise as a central element of aging healthily.

The benefits of remaining active go beyond physical health, touching on aspects like weight control, heart wellness, and mental state. Consistent workouts aid in weight regulation by enhancing metabolic rate and building muscle mass, which is essential as metabolism often decelerates with age. Heart wellness gains from regular exercise through better cardiac function, decreased blood pressure, and lower cholesterol figures. Additionally, the psychological health benefits of exercise, such as the release of endorphins that boost mood and the potential to enhance cognitive functions, emphasize the diverse advantages of physical fitness for individuals over 55.

Stretching exercises and strength training play a pivotal role in preserving functional abilities, which are essential for day-to-day tasks and autonomy. These exercises aid in conserving muscle mass and ensuring that joints remain supple, thus lessening the risk of falls and injuries, which are notable concerns for older adults. The inclusion of balance exercises further assists in averting falls, enabling individuals to sustain their preferred activities and independence for longer durations.

The social advantages of engaging in physical activity often don't obtain as much attention as the physical and mental wellness benefits, yet they are particularly impactful for older adults. Participating in physical exercises provides more than just health benefits; it opens gateways to social interaction and community involvement, which are essential for keeping a sense of belonging and purpose. Group fitness classes, walking clubs, and similar collective activities provide precious chances for interaction, forming new friendships, and renewing old ones. This community spirit is crucial, creating a supportive atmosphere where members can uplift and inspire one another, exchange stories, and share achievements. The social bonds formed through these engagements profoundly affect life's quality, offering a network of support and friendship.

Additionally, the significance of physical activity in combating feelings of solitude and isolation is noteworthy. For many seniors, especially those who've entered retirement or lost a partner, the frequency of social interactions can diminish. Participating in group-based exercise can counter this solitude, ensuring regular social exchanges and fostering inclusivity. This aspect is essential for mental well-being, as isolation is associated with various adverse health impacts, including heightened risks of depression, cognitive decline, and mortality. The companionship experienced in workout groups or associations not only makes exercising more enjoyable but also leads to a healthier, more interconnected existence. By including social elements into their workout routines, older adults can reap the dual benefits of improving their physical state while enriching their social life, showing how physical activity and social engagement are intertwined in contributing to a rewarding and dynamic life in later years.

Starting a fitness routine after 55 may appear challenging, but always remember, *"Slow and steady wins the race."* This approach is especially relevant when starting a journey toward improved health and fitness later in life. Beginning with manageable steps can result in substantial health advantages in the long run. It's important to discover fun activities that can be easily added to your daily routine, emphasizing the benefits of making exercise a consistent part of your life for long-term health. This systematic method of embracing a fitness routine highlights the importance of being patient and persistent, which are crucial for attaining long-term health results.

Accessible and simple exercises, like walking, can be especially attractive because of their convenience and gentle nature. These activities help people easily include physical exercise in their daily routines without requiring any particular equipment or facilities. Moreover, water-based exercises provide a low-impact alternative for individuals dealing with joint issues, offering a pleasant way to remain physically engaged. The part of technology, through wellness trackers and online classes, offers extra backing and inspiration, making it simpler for individuals to stay engaged with their wellness objectives.

Building upon the benefits of accessible and straightforward exercises, the insights from "Spark: The Revolutionary New Science of Exercise and the Brain" by Dr. John J. Ratey further amplify the importance of integrating physical activity into our daily lives. This book presents a compelling case for exercise not just as a tool for physical enhancement but as a critical component for mental health and cognitive function improvement.

Dr. Ratey, through extensive research, shows how activities such as walking and swimming can lead to significant improvements in brain function. He explains that exercise induces the release of various growth factors that help in the development of new neuronal connections, an aspect that is particularly beneficial as we age. These processes contribute to better memory, sharper focus, and more creativity, underscoring the intrinsic link between physical activity and brain health.

Moreover, "Spark" explores how regular engagement in physical exercise can act as a potent antidote to stress, anxiety, and depression. Dr. Ratey elaborates on how physical activity modulates the brain's stress response and elevates mood through complex neurological pathways, highlighting exercise as a powerful means of addressing common mental health challenges. Significantly, the book emphasizes that the mental health benefits of exercise are universal regardless of age or fitness level, providing a simple yet effective prescription for an overall healthier, happier brain.

Sufficient nutrition and hydration serve as the foundational elements that support the sanctity of physical fitness. Similar to how a robust foundation is necessary for a temple to endure the measure of time, optimal nutrition and balance are imperative for maintaining bodily health and vitality. A nourishment-rich diet functions as the structural components, reinforcing and constructing muscular fibers subsequent to each exercise session. Hydration, on the other hand, symbolizes the vital water that permeates this temple, guaranteeing the seamless function of every part. When combined, these components establish a haven of well-being, enabling the body to fully benefit from physical activity while remaining robust against the ravages of time. The interconnection of nutrition and hydration not only provides structural support but also elevates the spiritual dimension of wellness, thereby fostering a state of equilibrium that enriches the later stages of life.

Prioritizing physical health and fitness becomes increasingly significant in fostering a dynamic, energetic, and gratifying existence beyond the age of 55. By engaging in consistent physical activity, the elderly can experience increased mobility, diminished health hazards, and enhanced mental health. By placing physical activity and adopting a supportive lifestyle as top priorities, individuals can effectively confront the difficulties associated with aging while simultaneously benefiting from optimal health and well-being.

Customizing Your Exercise Routine

Creating a personalized exercise plan takes thoughtfulness, similar to cooking a unique dish tailored to one's tastes, nutritional needs, and the ingredients you have at hand. This customization requires self-awareness of bodily requirements, personal aims, and activities found enjoyable and maintainable. A well-crafted routine weighs several aspects, like present conditioning, medical concerns, lifestyle, and individual preferences. By paying attention to these aspects, you can develop a fitness regimen that not only achieves your goals but also is enjoyable, leading to long-term adherence and success.

Below are the essential steps to customizing your exercise routine to fit your unique needs and goals, ensuring a journey toward personal improvement that is both rewarding and sustainable:

1. Assess Your Fitness Level and Health Conditions

To customize your exercise routine effectively, first, evaluate your current physical condition and any health factors that might impact specific activities. This may involve focusing initially on low-impact options if joint issues are a concern or emphasizing cardiovascular workouts to boost heart health. Understanding your baseline (where you're starting from) enables setting practical objectives and selecting exercises that are guaranteed to be both safe and significantly beneficial. Consultation with a healthcare provider is also advisable, especially for pre-existing medical issues.

2. Define Your Fitness Goals

Setting clear objectives is the guiding light that will direct your fitness journey. Whether losing weight, building muscle, or enhancing flexibility and cardiovascular health, the goals you establish will shape the exercises in your routine. Targets should be specific, quantifiable, realistic, purposeful, and time-specific. For instance, running a 5k within three months is a specific, time-constrained goal. Your targets will directly affect picked exercises, workout intensity, and progress assessment.

3. Consider Your Lifestyle and Schedule

Your workout regimen is greatly influenced by your lifestyle and daily schedule. An individual with a 9-to-5 occupation may find lengthy gym periods challenging to commit to, whereas home exercises or brisk walks during lunch breaks could be more manageable. Reflecting on when you have stamina and time will help you decide the ideal times to incorporate activity into your day. Keep in mind that consistency is pivotal to fulfilling fitness goals, so opt for a period that you can stick to long term.

4. Choose Exercises You Enjoy

The foundation of any sustainable workout regime is enjoyment. If you love being outdoors, consider cycling, jogging, or hiking. If you prefer social environments, group classes or team sports might be more inspiring. For those who appreciate solitude, swimming, yoga, or home-based sessions could appeal. Mixing up your workouts with activities can keep things exciting and ward off boredom. The more you enjoy your exercise regimen, the more likely you are to stick to it.

5. Integrate Variety and Progression

To prevent plateaus in progress and maintain interest, your exercise routine should include a variety of activities that challenge different muscle groups and improve various aspects of fitness, such as strength, endurance, and flexibility. This approach also reduces the risk of overuse injuries. Progression is equally important as your fitness level improves. Increasing the intensity, duration, or frequency of your workouts will help you continue to advance toward your goals.

6. Listen to Your Body

A customized workout program needs to be flexible as well. Observe how your body reacts to various activities and modify as necessary. You may need to take it easy on certain days and push harder on others when you have more energy. Including days for rest in your routine helps you recover and avoid burnout. It is crucial for both safety and advancement to pay attention to your body's cues and modify your regimen as necessary.

7. Track Your Progress

Monitoring your growth is both inspiring and informative. Employing a journal, app, or fitness tracker to record your workouts, emotions, and any performance improvements allows you to evaluate what's effective and what necessitates adjustment in your schedule. This insight helps in fine-tuning your approach. Bear in mind, *"Rome wasn't built in a day."* Celebrate every milestone and progress, no matter how minor, to maintain high motivation levels. This age-old adage emphasizes the significance of patience and perseverance in reaching long-term fitness objectives by reminding us that significant accomplishments require time and consistent dedication.

8. Seek Professional Guidance

If you're feeling uncertain about how to begin or move forward, it might be helpful to consult with a fitness expert. A certified trainer can evaluate your fitness status, assist in setting objectives, and create a tailored workout regimen that takes into account your requirements, likes, and any restrictions you may have. They can also provide valuable, individualized feedback on your form and technique during exercises, reducing risks of injury while optimizing benefits from each workout.

Thus, customizing an exercise routine demands self-awareness, thoughtful planning, and consistent re-evaluation. By seriously considering your overall health, objectives, lifestyle, and what you find most motivating, an enjoyable, results-driven, and adaptive personalized fitness plan can be created that seamlessly fits into your busy routine while supporting your best well-being. Remember, the ideal routine comfortably slots into your daily life in a way that leaves you feeling energized. A rewarding and sustainable journey toward improved wellness is within reach with commitment and a customized approach tailored just for you.

Exploring the Harmony Between Mindfulness, Meditation, and Physical Well-being

In the quest for optimal health and vitality, the intertwined roles of mindfulness and meditation with physical fitness emerge as a balanced blend, offering a comprehensive approach to well-being. This exploration probes into how these mental practices meaningfully influence physical health, underlining a holistic view of wellness that encompasses both the body and the mind. The synergy between mindfulness, meditation, and physical fitness highlights the profound impact of mental states on physical health, offering insights into the practices that can foster a balanced and healthy lifestyle.

At the heart of this is the concept of mindfulness, which champions present moment awareness with an open and accepting attitude. This principle of being fully engaged with the present has far-reaching implications for physical health, enhancing the connection to one's physical being and paving the way for improved health outcomes. It suggests that the state of our mental health deeply influences our physical fitness and vice versa, proposing a more integrated approach to health and wellness.

The role of physical exercise in maintaining and improving health is well-documented, yet its effectiveness is significantly affected by the individual's mental state and focus. Mindfulness stands as a powerful enhancer of physical exercise, not only by ensuring a focused and engaged approach to fitness routines but also by transforming these activities into more fulfilling and immersive experiences. This mindful approach to exercise promotes a deeper connection with one's body, leading to safer and more effective workouts.

Similarly, meditation, often sought for mental tranquility, extends its benefits to physical health. Through its stress-reducing capabilities, meditation contributes to the prevention and management of stress-related diseases, showcasing the intrinsic link between mental calmness and physical health. The calming effect of meditation on the mind translates into tangible physical health benefits, including lower stress levels, reduced risk of chronic diseases, and enhanced resilience against physical and mental stressors.

Integrating mindfulness and meditation into a physical fitness regimen extends far beyond the simple inclusion of meditation periods within daily activities. This integration necessitates a holistic methodology whereby physical exercises are conducted with a mindful approach, centering attention on breathing patterns, bodily movements, and the sensations experienced during the activity. Such a strategy not only amplifies the physical advantages derived from exercising but also cultivates a deeper respect and comprehension of the body's abilities and requirements.

For instance, consider the practice of yoga, which inherently combines physical movement with mindful awareness. Participants are encouraged to focus on their breath as they move through various poses, enhancing both flexibility and mental clarity. This principle can be applied to other forms of exercise as well. During a run, for example, rather than letting the mind wander, one might concentrate on the rhythm of their breathing, the sensation of each foot striking against the ground, and the feeling of the wind against their skin. This mindfulness approach can transform a routine jog into a deeply personal experience of connection between body and environment.

The empirical evidence supporting the benefits of mindfulness and meditation on physical health is indeed compelling, underscoring their substantial positive impact across various health metrics. Research has consistently shown that these practices can lead to meaningful improvements in critical areas such as blood pressure, chronic pain management, sleep quality, and immune system performance, positioning them as key components of a holistic health and wellness strategy.

In terms of chronic pain, Mindfulness-Based Stress Reduction (MBSR) programs have been shown to be particularly effective. These programs, which typically involve guided meditation, body awareness exercises, and yoga, can help individuals change their relationship with pain. Instead of tensing up and exacerbating pain through resistance, patients learn to observe their pain with an accepting and nonjudgmental mindset, which can actually reduce the intensity of the pain.

Despite the clear benefits, incorporating mindfulness and meditation into a fitness routine is not without its challenges. The demands of daily life can make it difficult to find time and motivation for regular practice. Additionally, achieving the mental focus required for effective meditation and mindful exercise can be challenging for some individuals. However, the rewards of overcoming these obstacles are significant, offering a path to enhanced physical health, mental clarity, and emotional stability.

Consistency in Practice: The Pathway to Success

The need for consistency in all endeavors—whether they are artistic, scientific, athletic, or personal growth—cannot be overstated. A persistent dedication to practice and a daily presence pave the path to extraordinary accomplishments. The daily practice of a musician or the unrelenting experimentation of a scientist, for example, highlights the crucial role that constant effort plays in reaching expertise and invention.

The journey to mastery in any discipline is often long and fraught with challenges. These difficulties become stepping stones toward greatness because of the force of consistency. No matter what, making the daily commitment to practice fosters understanding and leads to progressive growth. This process sharpens abilities, expands knowledge, and lays the groundwork for success. A writer's discipline in penning a daily essay or an athlete's strict and regular training regimen demonstrates how consistency builds the foundation for achieving unprecedented levels of creativity and performance.

The importance of consistency is highlighted in the realm of sports, where athletes spend countless hours refining their skills. It is not merely the talent that distinguishes the greatest athletes but their unwavering dedication to consistent practice. This principle holds for both creative and scholarly activities and personal development. Significant improvement results from consistent practice on an instrument, regular engagement with difficult subjects, or persistent efforts to form new habits. The life-changing potential of consistency is best shown by the tales of Olympic swimmers who spend endless mornings in the water or famous scientists who devote decades to a single field of study.

The formation of discipline is one of the main advantages of consistency. The path from aspirations to achievement is paved with discipline, which regular practice strengthens. People who dedicate themselves to a consistent work schedule develop the self-control to overcome challenges and withstand distractions. This discipline gives all facets of life a stronger sense of direction and control, transcending the particular field of application. A martial artist's daily discipline or a top student's strict study routine shows how consistency fosters a greater ability for self-control and concentrated effort.

Moreover, consistency in practice fosters resilience. The path to success is rarely linear, marked instead by setbacks and failures. Consistent practice teaches individuals to view these challenges not as insurmountable obstacles but as opportunities for learning and growth. This resilience is crucial for long-term success, enabling individuals to persevere in adversity and strive toward their goals. The resilience built through repeated attempts and failures in innovation projects or athletic competitions illustrates the strength that consistency breeds, enabling individuals to bounce back stronger after setbacks.

However, maintaining consistency is not without its challenges. Life events can throw off habits, cause motivation to fade, and cause growth to stagnate. These are the times when consistency's actual worth becomes apparent. When people practice consistently, even in the face of difficulty, they show the dedication necessary to succeed. The enduring strength of consistency is demonstrated by the capacity to maintain a fitness routine through different stages of life or to pursue creative hobbies despite hardships in one's own life.

The key to developing consistency is establishing attainable, well-defined goals. Setting and achieving goals makes it simpler to stay motivated and focused. Establishing a regimen that is both demanding and long-lasting is also crucial. Overly complex routines might cause burnout, while too-easy routines could not present enough challenges to promote development. Well-balanced academic curricula and professional athletes' customized training regimens provide excellent examples of how vital calibrated challenges are to sustaining sustained interest. The enduring wisdom in the words of renowned motivational speaker Jim Rohn," Success *is neither magical nor mysterious. Success is the natural consequence of consistently applying fundamentals,"* rings especially true in the context of this discussion. The essence of success, whether in personal development, professional achievements, or creative endeavors, lies in the unwavering commitment to the fundamentals of consistent practice.

Therefore, a steadfast dedication to regular effort in diverse areas of life, from maintaining health and fitness to advancing personally and professionally, forms the foundation of achievement. This devotion to being present and working hard daily, even when faced with obstacles and without quick results, culminates in significant accomplishments. The path to betterment, characterized by steady perseverance and the ability to bounce back, highlights the influential role of regularity, showing that real success is not the result of intermittent attempts but rather the continuous dedication to advancement and development.

Chapter 14: Coping Mechanism

"Courage doesn't always roar. Sometimes courage is the quiet voice at the end of the day saying, 'I will try again tomorrow.'" Mary Anne Radmacher's words act as a beacon, guiding us through life's trials. They remind us that facing our fears and concerns is an inherent aspect of our existence. Life throws numerous challenges our way, testing our resolve and prompting us to introspect on our capabilities to handle life's unpredictable nature. This reflection is vital, pushing us to evaluate our resilience and adaptability in the face of adversity.

It's critical to grasp the core of our fears. These feelings encourage us to look further by pointing out possible dangers or unsolved problems. Clarity is achieved by examining the origin of our worries and differentiating between real worries and worries that are heightened by outside pressures. This degree of self-examination is essential for developing a thorough understanding of our concerns and assisting us in sensibly managing our emotions. It gives us the means to distinguish between legitimate fears and those that distort reality, pointing us in the direction of logical reactions.

People from history, such as Frida Kahlo and Winston Churchill, demonstrate the effectiveness of facing fears head-on. Churchill famously remarked, *"Fear is a reaction. Courage is a decision,"* in reference to the difficult challenge of guiding Britain through World War II. Being brave is a choice. His leadership in the face of extreme danger and uncertainty highlights the value of making brave decisions despite widespread fears. Similar to this, Frida Kahlo used her work to powerfully express her identity and truth despite experiencing physical and emotional agony. Her work expresses an unwavering exploration of the self through embracing her concerns and obstacles and transforming them into meaningful artistic statements. These individuals show how tackling our fears and being well-informed about their causes may result in remarkably strong resilience and creativity.

Being honest about our fears without passing judgment on them is a significant step toward self-awareness. This act of acceptance is proof of our fortitude rather than a sign of weakness. By accepting our fears, we discover our inner power and come to understand that these feelings are only parts of the larger human experience. This insight gives us the courage to face our worries head-on and cultivates a sense of control and assurance that they are only obstacles we must conquer rather than what defines us.

The diversity of coping strategies to deal with fears is a reflection of the uniqueness of our experiences. However, their success mostly rests on their capacity to provide consolation and a change of viewpoint. Developing coping mechanisms can be life-changing, enabling us to confront our fears constructively. These approaches help us become masters of our emotional terrain, giving us the stability we need to face life's challenges with confidence and grace while strengthening our sense of autonomy over our emotions.

The act of choosing and applying coping mechanisms reinforces our sense of autonomy over our internal landscape. It's a declaration that, while we may not have control over external events, we hold the reins when it comes to our reactions and attitudes. This autonomy is powerful because it gives one a sense of control over circumstances that at first seem to be ruled by uncertainty or fear. This empowerment changes the way we view challenges, turning them from overwhelming dangers to doable parts of the journey. It enables us to take a proactive attitude to life, actively confronting our fears instead of allowing them to control us. In the end, this encourages a closer relationship with ourselves as we align our decisions and behaviors with our beliefs and objectives, overcoming life's obstacles with assurance and fortitude.

The life story of Aron Ralston is a perfect example of how coping skills may turn fear into an opportunity for personal development. A life-threatening predicament struck the enthusiastic outdoorsman and explorer Ralston in 2003 when he was canyoneering alone in southeast Utah when a boulder fell, trapping his arm. He was stuck for five days before he terrifyingly decided to amputate his own arm with a dull multi-tool in order to get out and call for help.

Ralston's story stands as a powerful demonstration of the human ability to face and overcome extreme adversity and fears. Throughout his ordeal, he depended on diverse coping strategies, such as mindfulness, to uphold his psychological well-being and execute the challenging choices essential for his existence. His narrative subsequently shared in his publication "Between a Rock and a Hard Place" and the movie "127 Hours," showcases how fortitude, mindfulness, and the capacity to coolly evaluate one's circumstances can result in remarkable displays of bravery.

Ralston didn't allow his tragic experience to dampen his sense of adventure after he recovered. Rather than giving up, he kept doing outdoor sports and even turned into a motivational speaker, using his experience to encourage others to face their fears and meet life's challenges head-on with courage and optimism. Ralston's journey stands as an example of how facing our worst fears and using constructive coping mechanisms can not only help us overcome immediate challenges but also significantly and favorably alter our lives.

The journey toward embracing our vulnerabilities and leveraging them as strengths forge a path of profound connection and understanding with those around us. This recognition of our common humanity strengthens the ties that bind us together and lessens our sense of loneliness. The essence of who we are changes when we move through the different terrains of life and come across changes in our hopes and fears. This progression, characterized by the shifts from the energy of youth to the reflection of our older years, offers a variety of chances and challenges for growth and development on a personal level. Maintaining a healthy balance in life requires that we acknowledge these changes and modify our coping and growing techniques accordingly. This kind of adaptation guarantees that we continue to be robust and alive, able to thrive despite the unavoidable changes that come with life.

Effective Coping Strategies for Well-being

Beginning on this continuous journey of growth necessitates an arsenal of positive coping mechanisms after 55. These strategies, ranging from the tranquility found in mindfulness meditation to the structured progress achieved by setting attainable goals, guide us through the complexities of life.

Integrating these practices into our daily routines not only alters our perception of and reaction to stress but also enriches our lives with a deeper sense of fulfillment and balance. By embracing these mechanisms, we harness the power to not just endure but thrive, transforming our lives in ways that resonate with meaning, joy, and inner peace.

Below are the coping mechanisms:

1. Mindfulness Meditation

This practice has become renowned in the Western world for its significant influence on diminishing stress and boosting overall wellness. Activities vary from guided exercises, where an instructor guides you through a sequence of calming visualizations, to Mindfulness-Based Stress Reduction (MBSR) programs that merge meditation with yoga and psychoeducation. These exercises aid in fostering a nonjudgmental consciousness of the current moment, motivating individuals to escape the cycle of persistent stress and detrimental thought loops. The advantages of regular mindfulness exercises reach beyond instant relaxation, aiding in long-term enhancements in emotional stability, focus, and even pain relief.

2. Regular Physical Activity

The World Health Organization recommends adults engage in 150 minutes of moderate-intensity aerobic activity weekly. Such endeavors not only elevate cardiovascular well-being but also play a crucial role in warding off chronic conditions like diabetes and heart disease. The psychological gains are just as vital, with physical activity acting as a natural antidote to anxiety that betters stress coping by improving the body's stress response. This improvement is due to the heightened heart rate, which may cause an uptick in neurohormone production like norepinephrine that betters cognitive function and mood, easing the brain's reaction to stress.

3. Healthy Eating Habits

The complex interconnection between what we eat and how we feel has gained increasing evidence, accentuating the interplay between dietary choices and mental condition. Essential nutrients such as omega-3 fatty acids, antioxidants, and vitamins supplied by a balanced dietary pattern are pivotal for brain health, impacting mood-modulating neurotransmitters like serotonin and dopamine. Furthermore, research on the intricate gut-brain communication network known as the gut-brain axis proposes that intestinal wellness can sway emotions and psychological health. By incorporating probiotic-rich meals like yogurt into one's sustenance plan, gut microbial diversity may be bolstered, further contributing to emotional resilience and stress adaptation. In addition, regular exercise and stress-reducing activities can aid mood elevation for many by encouraging relaxation and calm focus, providing mental respite during challenging intervals.

4. Adequate Rest

The importance of sleep in emotional and physical health cannot be overstated. Studies indicate that adults require 7-9 hours of sleep per night for optimal functioning. The pre-sleep routine is equally critical, where activities like reading or taking a warm bath can signal to the body that it's time to wind down. Creating a sleep environment in the bedroom with bedding, a cool room temperature, and minimal noise can further enhance our rest. Furthermore, reducing caffeine intake in the hours preceding sleep can prevent interruptions during sleep. By incorporating these practices, not only does the body have the opportunity to repair and re-energize during the night, but it also boosts cognitive functions like decision-making and problem-solving abilities, better preparing us to tackle life's challenges with resilience. This holistic approach toward rest highlights its vital role as a foundation for maintaining a healthy lifestyle, ensuring we are rejuvenated and ready for whatever comes our way the next day.

5. Social Support

Spending time with family and friends, engaging in societal events, or becoming part of groups that reflect one's hobbies can reinforce their circle of support. Interacting socially fosters a sense of inclusion and can serve as a significant source of solace and assurance in challenging periods. The heart of this concept is captured in an ancient saying that goes, *"A friend in need is a friend indeed."* This proverb emphasizes the vital role that friendship and community play in our lives, stressing how they provide a safety net that helps us overcome obstacles in life with more self-assurance and fortitude.

6. Creative Expression

Artistic activities offer a distinct avenue for processing and articulating emotions, whether through painting, crafting, writing poetry, or playing an instrument. These pursuits can divert attention from stress to self-expression, acting as a therapeutic mechanism for emotional exploration and recovery. Diving into the artistic process can also encourage a state of 'flow,' where time appears to halt, and one's concerns dissipate. This engagement not only nourishes the soul but also boosts cognitive skills and problem-solving abilities, improving overall mental agility. Regular participation in artistic endeavors can thus be a profound source of happiness and self-development, making life richer with purpose and enthusiasm.

7. Time Management

While setting schedules and prioritizing to-do lists are helpful for keeping tasks on track, strict routines often overlook life's unpredictable nature. Both productivity and leisure are essential for well-being, but balance comes through flexibility. As Benjamin Franklin once wisely noted, "By failing to prepare, you are preparing to fail." Thoughtful time management acknowledges life's ebbs and flows, allocating moments for work as well as rest yet leaving room for improvisation. By treating our days with care but not rigidity and respecting humanity's need for both accomplishment and relaxation, we can face each challenge and discovery with greater calm.

8. Deep Breathing Exercises

Practices like the 4-7-8 technique or box breathing can be seamlessly incorporated into daily routines, offering immediate stress alleviation. These techniques trigger the body's inherent relaxation response, decelerating the heart rate and reducing blood pressure, providing a swift and accessible way to cope with moments of intense stress. Particularly, the 4-7-8 breathing technique, formulated by Dr Andrew Weil, involves silently inhaling through the nose for 4 seconds, holding the breath for 7 seconds, and forcefully exhaling through the mouth for 8 seconds. This breathing pattern is effective in lessening anxiety and aiding individuals to regain a composed and focused demeanor, especially in stressful situations. Making these exercises a routine part of one's day can significantly boost one's capacity to stay poised amidst life's challenges.

9. Setting Realistic Goals

Setting specific, attainable objectives and dividing them into manageable steps can encourage progress and reduce the feeling of being swamped. Acknowledging minor triumphs along the path can elevate confidence and provide a continual sense of accomplishment, keeping stress at a distance. A historical figure who embodied this approach was Thomas Edison. His journey to invent the electric light bulb comprised setting and accomplishing numerous step-by-step goals. Edison's renowned saying, "I have not failed. I've just found 10,000 ways that won't work," mirrors his attitude toward gradual advancement and learning from each attempt, regardless of its scale. This systematic approach not only culminated in significant discoveries but also exemplified the efficacy of perseverance and establishing realistic, stepwise objectives in surmounting obstacles and achieving success.

These mechanisms equip individuals to navigate the stresses and transitions accompanying aging, not merely by enduring but by excelling. They promote an existence lived intentionally, where hurdles are approached with resilience and grace, and each day is enriched with significance. By integrating these strategies into daily life, individuals can ensure that their later years are distinguished by vitality, joy, and a profound sense of contentment. Embracing this path with an open heart and a proactive attitude can transform the years following 55 into some of the most fulfilling years of one's life, brimming with opportunities for self-discovery and happiness.

In essence, by incorporating positive coping mechanisms into daily life, individuals can journey through the challenges of life after 55 with grace, resilience, and joy. These practices contribute to overall well-being, fostering physical health, emotional resilience, social connections, and a sense of purpose. By embracing self-care, nurturing relationships, pursuing meaningful activities, and cultivating gratitude, individuals can create a fulfilling and rewarding life in their later years.

Chapter 15: Seeking Professional Help

Therapy and counseling stand as critical resources for individuals confronting emotional, mental, or psychological hurdles. These professional services offer a non-judgmental space where individuals can freely express their thoughts and feelings. By engaging in this process, people can begin to understand and address the root causes of their distress, which is a crucial step toward recovery. This understanding enables individuals to tackle their issues with greater clarity and effectiveness.

"The only journey is the journey within."

-Rainer Maria Rilke

This quote emphasizes the importance of internal exploration and healing that therapy facilitates.

Emotional well-being forms the foundation for overall health, mirroring how physical health is just as essential. Therapy and counseling play indispensable roles in maintaining mental health, offering a confidential forum for clients to explore feelings. Early intervention in emotional and psychological concerns deters worsening, promoting a more stable and fulfilling life. Through these supportive services, individuals gain an understanding of their emotional state, cultivating a healthier psychological landscape. *"A problem shared is a problem halved,"* goes the proverb, highlighting the therapeutic value of sharing one's struggles.

A significant advantage of therapy is that it develops coping mechanisms. These techniques empower handling life's tests with resilience, reducing the impacts of anxiety, stress, and depression. Additionally, these coping strategies prepare people for future stressors, promoting enduring fortitude. Therapy and counseling thus equip individuals with skills to navigate life's ups and downs more smoothly.

Accessibility to therapy and counseling is crucial to their effectiveness. As digital platforms become more prevalent, online counseling sessions and mental health applications are simplifying the process for individuals to seek assistance. This transition toward digital accessibility ensures that support is accessible to those who may have previously been unable to access traditional face-to-face sessions due to geographical, financial, or time constraints. The democratization of access to mental health resources represents a pivotal progression in rendering mental health care universally reachable.

Another vital aspect is the continuous improvement and adaptation of therapeutic methods to meet diverse needs. With the progress in psychological research, counseling and therapy sessions are becoming more customized to individual encounters. This individualization ensures that therapy is not a one-size-fits-all solution but a subtle approach that recognizes and deals with the distinct challenges and backgrounds of each person. As therapy becomes more inclusive and adaptable, it further augments its ability to support a broader range of mental health needs, nurturing a more resilient and mentally robust society.

Therapy and counseling prove highly beneficial in nurturing interpersonal relationships. By cultivating self-awareness and regulating emotions, interactions improve through enhanced listening and open communication, leading to healthier, more constructive bonds. This relationship-strengthening ripples outward to enhance mental and emotional wellness, highlighting our social ties' influence on individual welfare. Such services impart strategies for resolving conflicts peaceably and building stronger connections with loved ones.

For example, consider an individual hesitant to share needs for fear of rejection. Counseling equips them with tools to express feelings assertively. Progressively, they articulate needs and emotions more confidently within relationships, fostering understanding and intimacy. This real-world application demonstrates how heightened emotional intelligence and communication competence directly boost relationship quality.

The journey through counseling promotes individual growth and self-awareness. Individuals are urged to ponder their encounters, recognizing strengths and areas for enhancement. This introspective procedure encourages goal establishment and the pursuit of favorable transformation, fostering personal evolution. Consequently, therapy and guidance not only tackle current obstacles but also aid individuals in realizing their complete potential.

Support during notable life shifts is another crucial facet of counseling and therapy. Alterations such as professional transitions, entering or leaving relationships, and coping with bereavement can be deeply unsettling. Professional assistance enables individuals to adjust to these alterations, discovering balance and stability amidst turbulent periods. This direction is priceless in ensuring that transitions are handled healthily and constructively.

The societal viewpoint regarding mental health care is progressing, partly due to heightened awareness of the advantages of therapy and counseling. As more individuals divulge their affirmative experiences, seeking aid becomes more embraced and encouraged. This transformation contributes to a community where mental health maintenance is recognized as a normal and vital element of overall well-being preservation. Prominent figures and celebrities openly discussing their mental health journeys have played a noteworthy role in this shift.

For example, when a renowned personality recounts their story of how counseling aided them in conquering a period of despondency or anxiety, it can motivate others to seek assistance for their own challenges. This visibility assists in demystifying therapy and counseling, demonstrating that mental health struggles do not discriminate based on stature or triumph. Through persistent dialogue and instruction, we can further diminish stigma and bolster mental wellness for all. Public campaigns and mental health consciousness endeavors, utilizing social media and alternative platforms, also make notable contributions to this cultural transformation, emphasizing more than ever that mental well-being is a fundamental element of overall health.

Nurturing Mental Well-being in the Golden Years

While the core benefits of therapy and counseling have been established above, exploring further into how these services cater to nuanced needs after the age of 55 provides a deeper understanding of their value.

1. Fostering Adaptability to Technological Advancements

In an era when technologies rapidly evolve, many seniors find themselves struggling to keep pace with modern communication modes, information access, and entertainment platforms. Such experiences can lead to sensations of isolation or frustration. Therapy aims to build assurance with digital tools, not solely to strengthen bonds with loved ones through connectivity but also to explore apps and services designed for mental health, physical activities, and cognitive engagement. This assistance helps to bridge the digital divide, allowing elders to reap the abundant resources accessible online, from telehealth to educational platforms. As a result, they become more self-reliant and engaged in a world that progressively operates digitally, mitigating risks like social disengagement and promoting a more active lifestyle.

2. Encouraging Lifelong Learning and Intellectual Engagement

Maintaining cognitive agility and curiosity is crucial for well-being. Therapists motivate individuals to participate in lifelong discovering opportunities, such as taking classes, attending workshops, or pursuing novel interests. This intellectual involvement fosters a sense of achievement and satisfaction, contributing to general welfare. Moreover, by stimulating their brains through new avenues, seniors may potentially delay cognitive decline and boost life satisfaction. Involvement in such activities also provides chances for social interaction, further enriching lives and expanding social networks.

3. Addressing Late-Life Career Transitions

Some individuals choose to continue working or embark on new career ventures after 55. These decisions can bring about a mix of excitement and uncertainty. Counseling provides a venue to deeply ponder these career changes, easing strain while anchoring work revisions with inner motives and values. This profound reflection could result in rediscovery as individuals unearth novel interests or reawaken dormant passions, defining their further years not simply as retirement but as rebirth. Practitioners also facilitate navigating challenges balancing work with wellness considerations, family responsibilities, and leisure, guaranteeing a holistic life planning approach.

4. Supporting Sexual Health and Intimacy

Sexual health and intimacy remain important aspects of life for many older adults, yet these topics are often overlooked in discussions about aging. Therapy can offer a risk-free space to handle questions and worries concerning sexual wellness, intimacy, and evolving relationship dynamics, advancing a healthy and fulfilling personal life. By confronting social stigma and personal anxiety surrounding aging and sexuality, therapy helps people and couples maintain or rediscover physical and emotional intimacy. This process can strengthen bonds, boost self-esteem, and heighten overall quality of life, highlighting the importance of addressing sexual health as part of comprehensive care In later lIfe.

5. Navigating the Digital Age of Social Connection

The shift toward more screen-based socializing has significantly changed how individuals communicate, presenting both risks and rewards for older adults. Counselors can educate people on safely and productively utilizing online networking platforms while also stressing the continued importance of face-to-face exchanges to boost emotional and social health. Providing this guidance is pivotal in assisting older adults in overcoming technological apprehension, allowing them to remain in touch with loved ones from afar, engage with virtual interest groups, and participate in community events that may now take place digitally. Moreover, therapists can suggest ways to balance virtual interactions with real-world connections, making certain digital tools augment rather than replace meaningful human interaction.

6. Preparing for Multigenerational Living

Multigenerational living arrangements are becoming increasingly prevalent, offering both advantages and tests. Therapy can aid individuals in preparing for and adapting to cohabiting with family members of diverse generations, facilitating interaction, establishing boundaries, and cultivating a harmonious domestic environment. Counselors can provide useful tools for negotiating space, privacy, and daily routines, which are critical for reducing clashes. They are also able to help families see each other's perspectives and needs from a place of empathy and strengthen bonds within a shared living arrangement.

7. Enhancing Physical Health Through Mental Well-being

While the interplay between psychological and physical wellness has long been evident, therapy provides aging individuals valuable support in cultivating beneficial habits, dealing with ongoing illnesses, and preserving flexibility and autonomy. This comprehensive methodology underscores how inner peace influences outer health. Counselors can advantageously affect medical consequences by tackling unease, despair, or strain, prompting activities that nourish both body and mind. Furthermore, establishing achievable wellness targets and marking victories propels seniors to continue lively, healthful routines, further augmenting their joy of living. Meanwhile, acknowledging limits and accepting what cannot be changed is also important for well-being. A balanced approach integrating physical, mental, and spiritual health can help people age successfully.

8. Cultivating a Positive Relationship with Aging

Society often portrays aging in an unfortunate manner, yet counseling can aid persons in cultivating a more optimistic perspective of this natural process. By centering on the pleasures, knowledge, and possibilities that aging may offer, therapy inspires a healthier, more hopeful attitude regarding the passing years. Professionals can dispute age-related assumptions and assist clients in recognizing the significance of their life experiences, fostering a feeling of achievement and accomplishment. This good view of aging may rouse older adults to embrace their age confidently, actively search out fresh adventures, and appreciate the exclusive benefits of this life period.

9. Contributing to Community and Legacy Building

As people age, their legacy and the lasting impression they leave on their community come to mind. Therapists can assist in pinpointing impactful ways to volunteer, mentor, and get involved through values-driven opportunities to make a difference. This guidance not only enriches older adults' lives but also fortifies social bonds and cultivates intergenerational relationships. Furthermore, taking part in such engagements can offer a feeling of significance and satisfaction, strengthening one's sense of belonging and role in enhancing society.

10. Embracing Spirituality and Existential Reflection

For many people, the later stages of life spark a deeper introspection about spirituality and life's deepest questions. Counseling can help facilitate this journey, aiding individuals in attaining inner serenity, motivation, and bonds through spiritual practices or philosophical thought. This process can profoundly reassure, delivering solace and a feeling of connectedness over time. Moreover, it can empower people to live out their remaining days intentionally and gracefully, choosing meanings reflecting what they value most. In these explorations, counselors assist individuals in developing a richer self-understanding and sense of place in the world, enhancing how they experience aging.

Therefore, as individuals face the complexities of life after 55, therapy and counseling can provide multifaceted support and guidance. Addressing both the traditional challenges linked to aging as well as the less discussed but equally important aspects of living a purposeful life during these years, mental healthcare plays a pivotal role. Beyond coping with changes and losses, therapy enriches the golden years, empowering older adults to discover new horizons, sustain meaningful bonds, and celebrate the journey of aging with dignity, intention, and joy.

A Practical Guide to Finding a Therapist or Counselor

Getting on the journey to find a therapist or counselor that matches one's needs can seem daunting. This guide aims to simplify the process, providing clear and actionable steps to connect with a mental health professional who can offer the support and guidance needed. Moreover, this guide emphasizes the value of self-reflection and proactive exploration in making an informed choice, highlighting the variety of resources accessible to help in the search. It seeks to simplify the process, making mental health support more obtainable to those requiring it, guaranteeing individuals feel empowered to initiate healing.

Understanding Your Needs

Before commencing your search, it's crucial to have a clear understanding of why you seek assistance. Are you managing feelings of sadness, worry, relationship issues, or perhaps life transitions feeling overwhelming? Distinguishing your major concerns will help narrow down your exploration to specialists concentrating on addressing those specific problems. This introspective step is not just about finding any therapist but about finding the appropriate one for you, one who aligns with your personal journey and aims. It's the foundation upon which the therapeutic relationship is constructed, ensuring that the therapy offered is applicable and tailored to your specific needs.

Researching Therapists and Counselors

1. Utilize Online Directories and Resources

Many professional organizations offer online directories to help you find therapists and counselors in your area. These directories often allow you to filter your search by location, specialty, and insurance acceptance. Exploring these resources can also provide insights into the therapist's philosophy, approach, and areas of expertise, giving you a comprehensive view before making contact. This step is instrumental in creating a shortlist of potential therapists who are not just licensed professionals but also resonate with your personal criteria for selection.

2. Consider Teletherapy Options:

If geographical limitations or mobility issues are a concern, teletherapy might be a suitable option. Many therapists offer sessions via phone or video calls, providing flexibility and convenience. This mode of therapy has gained popularity, offering the same level of confidentiality and effectiveness as in-person sessions. It opens up a wider range of options, allowing you to find a therapist who might not be in your immediate vicinity but is the perfect fit for your needs.

Evaluating Credentials and Specializations

Therapists and counselors come from different backgrounds and specialties. Understanding the various credentials, such as Licensed Clinical Social Worker (LCSW), Psychologist (PhD or PsyD), Licensed Professional Counselor (LPC), and Psychiatrist (MD), can help you decide which type of professional might best meet your needs. Additionally, many professionals specialize in specific therapeutic approaches or issues, such as Cognitive-Behavioral Therapy (CBT) for anxiety or family therapy for relationship challenges. This knowledge not only aids in matching with a therapist suited to address your concerns but also ensures that the treatment approach aligns with your comfort level and expectations. It underlines the importance of personal fit in therapy beyond just qualifications and titles.

Initial Contact and Consultation

1. Making the First Contact

Once you have a list of potential therapists, reach out to them via phone or email. Many therapists offer a brief initial consultation at no charge, allowing you to ask questions and get a feel for their approach and personality. This first interaction can be a valuable indicator of how comfortable and supported you'll feel in sessions. It's an opportunity to express your needs and hear directly from the therapist how they can help you navigate your concerns.

2 Ask Important Questions

Use the initial consultation to ask about their experience with your specific concerns, their therapeutic approach, session length, frequency, and fees. This is also a good time to inquire about insurance coverage or sliding scale options if cost is a concern. Asking detailed questions not only clarifies the practical aspects of therapy but also helps establish expectations, laying the groundwork for a transparent and productive therapeutic relationship. This step is crucial in ensuring that there are no surprises down the line and that you feel fully informed and comfortable moving forward.

3 Assessing the Fit

The relationship between you and your therapist is crucial for effective therapy. After the initial consultation, reflect on how comfortable you felt with the therapist and whether their approach aligns with your preferences and needs. It's okay to consult with several therapists before deciding on the best fit for you. A strong therapeutic alliance is fundamental to the success of therapy, influencing the openness and honesty of your interactions. Feeling understood and validated by your therapist is key to fostering an environment where meaningful change can occur.

Practical Considerations

1. Location and Accessibility

Consider the therapist's location and whether the office is easily accessible to you. If you're considering teletherapy, discuss how sessions will be conducted and ensure you have the privacy and technology needed. These logistical details play a significant role in your therapy experience, affecting convenience and your ability to attend sessions consistently. Ensuring that these aspects fit within your lifestyle and preferences can enhance your commitment and engagement with the therapeutic process.

2. Scheduling

Make sure the therapist's availability aligns with your schedule. Consistent sessions are important for effective therapy. Regular appointments contribute to a structured therapeutic process, allowing for gradual progress and deepening the therapist-client relationship. Flexibility in scheduling can also alleviate potential stressors, making therapy a more integrated and manageable part of your life.

Making the Most of Therapy

Once you've chosen a therapist and started sessions, it's important to engage in the process actively. Be open and honest in your sessions, and remember that progress can take time. If, after several sessions, you feel that the fit is not right, it's acceptable to reassess and potentially look for another therapist who better meets your needs. This engagement is a two-way street, requiring the therapist's expertise and your willingness to explore and work through difficult areas. It's a partnership where both parties contribute to achieving the desired outcomes, emphasizing the collaborative nature of therapy.

Finding the right therapist or counselor at the age of 55 or beyond is a highly personal process that can significantly impact your mental health journey. By clearly understanding your needs, researching options, evaluating potential therapists, and assessing fit, you can establish a supportive and therapeutic relationship that fosters growth and well-being. Remember, seeking help is a sign of strength, and finding the proper support is crucial to achieving mental health and happiness, especially during this transformative period of life. This journey, while it may require effort and patience, is a profound investment in your overall quality of life, offering a path toward healing and self-discovery as you navigate the complexities and opportunities that come with aging.

"As we age, seeking support is not a sign of weakness but a mark of wisdom. It is the brave who ask for guidance, for they understand that growth is an ongoing process."

-Carl Jung

Conclusion

Traveling through life beyond 55, this book acts as a guide, directing us through various challenges and opportunities. From accepting changes to exploring health, societal views, and financial stability, we traverse paths of senior living with open hearts and a positive outlook. Our exploration reveals not only the obstacles of aging but also the limitless possibilities that enrich this phase of life. Each chapter, a milestone, lights the many-sided aging experience, demonstrating that with every change comes a chance for growth, reflection, and newfound joys.

Embracing change emerges as a central theme, teaching us it's not about loss but fresh starts. It encourages us to view our health differently, to adjust to social shifts, to revisit our financial plans, and to treasure the connections that support us. Welcoming change is like opening the door to a world of possibilities, where every step taken is a step toward thriving in the years that follow 55.

Discussing health concerns, the book places a strong emphasis on the preventive management of both physical and mental well-being. It advocates for regular checkups, mental wellness, and participation in activities that strengthen the body and spirit. This emphasis on health as a valuable asset becomes especially significant in later years, serving as the foundation for a fulfilling life. Through this perspective, health is not just about avoiding illness but about enhancing the quality of every day.

In the chapters on aging and society, we've confronted ageism, challenged societal norms, and celebrated the evolving story of aging as a period rich with valuable contributions. This part of the journey invites us to defy stereotypes and proudly represent our age, recognizing the depth of wisdom, experience, and unique perspectives we offer. It's a call to view aging not as a decline but as a continuation of life's vibrant essence, enriched with stories of resilience and accomplishment.

Financial uncertainties often cloud our senior years, yet the book provides a road map for confidently steering through these challenges. By tackling financial concerns directly, it lays the foundation for a future where financial security empowers us to pursue our dreams without restriction. This discussion goes beyond mere budgeting, touching on the essential aspect of financial peace of mind as a crucial ingredient for a life lived fully and without limitations.

Our discussion on loneliness and social isolation highlights the vital Importance of human connection. It prompts us to build and nurture relationships, establish strong support networks, and engage in community life. In doing so, we discover that fears of isolation are dispelled by the warmth of companionship and shared experiences, reminding us that the bonds we create and maintain are at the core of a fulfilled life.

Family and relationships, as explored in the book, are shown to develop with age, requiring us to adapt with empathy, effective communication, and an open heart. This section is a guide for facing the changing dynamics within families and friendships, showing that these changes are opportunities for deeper understanding and connection. It highlights those relationships, like life, are ever-evolving, with each stage offering unique lessons and joys.

This book not only maps the course through the later years of life but also celebrates the journey. It assures us that beyond 55 lies a vast range of possibilities for discovery, passion, and fulfillment. As we turn the final page of our lives, we have the information and motivation to confidently begin the new chapter of our lives, seizing the many opportunities ahead with hope and purpose. Life after 55 is shown as a journey rather than a finale, one filled with opportunity where each experience, hardship, and victory adds to the richness and splendor of our existence.

"In the end, it's not the years in your life that count. It's the life in your years." - Abraham Lincoln.

May this quote be a beacon on your journey, a constant source of inspiration for the rich and dynamic life that's possible at any age. Each year is a treasure, offering us the chance to bring more meaning, vibrancy, and happiness into our life story. Writing this guide on navigating the complexities of life after 55, I aim to encourage you to greet each day as a repository of endless opportunities, inviting you to reshape the concept of aging with elegance, intent, and a relentless passion for life.

This journey through the pages has been as much a revelation for me as I hope it has been for you. In writing this book, I've probed into the heart of what it means to age, discovering along the way that the later years of our lives are not just a time to reflect on the past but an extraordinary opportunity to embrace the present and look to the future with excitement and optimism.

Let's step into this next chapter together, armed with the knowledge that our senior years can be some of the most rewarding and fulfilling times of our lives. Here's to exploring, learning, and loving with the same fervor we had at half our age, proving that, truly, the best is yet to come.

To all who walked this path beside me, thank you. May you find pleasure in each moment, peace with each step, and a profound sense of meaning lighting your life beyond 55.

www.ingramcontent.com/pod-product-compliance
Lightning Source LLC
Chambersburg PA
CBHW071246150726
48001CB00018B/158